Twenty Famous Lawyers

John Hostettler

Twenty Famous Lawyers
John Hostettler

Published 2013 by
Waterside Press
Sherfield Gables
Sherfield on Loddon
Hook, Hampshire
United Kingdom RG27 0JG

Telephone +44(0)1256 882250
E-mail enquiries@watersidepress.co.uk
Online catalogue WatersidePress.co.uk

ISBN 978-1-904380-98-6 (Paperback)
ISBN 978-1-908162-53-3 (Kindle/Epub ebook)
ISBN 978-1-908162-54-0 (Adobe ebook)

Copyright © 2013 This work is the copyright of John Hostettler. All intellectual property and associated rights are hereby asserted and reserved by him in full compliance with UK, European and international law. No part of this book may be copied, reproduced, stored in any retrieval system or transmitted in any form or by any means, including in hard copy or via the internet, without the prior written permission of the publishers to whom all such rights have been assigned worldwide.

Cover design © 2013 Waterside Press. Design by www.gibgob.com.

Main UK distributor Gardners Books, 1 Whittle Drive, Eastbourne, East Sussex, BN23 6QH. Tel: +44 (0)1323 521777; sales@gardners.com; www.gardners.com

North American distribution Ingram Book Company, One Ingram Blvd, La Vergne, TN 37086, USA. Tel: (+1) 615 793 5000; inquiry@ingramcontent.com

Cataloguing-In-Publication Data A catalogue record for this book can be obtained from the British Library.

Printed by Lightning Source.

e-book *Twenty Famous Lawyers* is available as an ebook and also to subscribers of Myilibrary, Dawsonera, ebrary, and Ebscohost.

Twenty Famous Lawyers

John Hostettler

❈ WATERSIDE PRESS

Contents

About the Author   vi
Preface   vii

1 **Clarence Darrow**...13
   Freedom and Humanity

2 **Edward Carson**..25
   Strong Man of Politics and the Law

3 **William Howe and Abraham Hummel**...........................39
   Tricksters and Criminals

4 **Matthew Hale**...47
   Judge, Jurist, Writer, Reformer

5 **Marcus Tullius Cicero**...57
   Birth of the Rule of Law

6 **Henry Brougham**..65
   Glitz of Cannes to the Calm of the Woolsack

7 **John Adams**..73
   Constitutional Draftsman and President

8 **Helena Kennedy**..81
   Parliament, Court and College

9 **Norman Birkett**...87
   One of the 'Great Advocates'

10 **Jeremy Bentham**...95
   Utility, Punishment and Law

11 **Geoffrey Robertson** 105
    Rights, Romans and Regicides

12 **Abraham Lincoln** 113
    Law, Politics and Civil War

13 **Edward Coke**. 121
    Champion of the Common Law

14 **Thomas Jefferson** 131
    Visionary and Founding Father

15 **Shami Chakrabati** 141
    Equality, Respect and Human Rights

16 **James Fitzjames Stephen** 147
    Codes and Colonies

17 **Edward Marshall Hall**. 161
    Forensic Skills and Spell-binding Eloquence

18 **Gareth Peirce** 171
    Public Works, Private Life

19 **Alfred Denning** 177
    People's Judge and an Unlikely Celebrity

20 **Cesare Beccaria**. 185
    Crusader Against Torture

Select Bibliography   191
Index   199

About the Author

John Hostettler is an expert on English legal history and has written several biographies of eminent legal figures. He was a practising solicitor in London for 35 years as well as undertaking political and civil liberties cases in Nigeria, Germany and Aden.

His other books include: *Garrow's Law* (2012); *Dissenters, Radicals and Blasphemers* (2012); *Champions of the Rule of Law* (2011); *Sir William Garrow: His Life Times and Fight for Justice* (2010) (with Richard Braby); *Thomas Erskine and Trial by Jury* (re-issued in 2010); *Cesare Beccaria* (2010); *A History of Criminal Justice in England and Wales* (2009); *Fighting for Justice: The History and Origins of Adversary Trial* (2006); *The Criminal Jury Old and New* (2004); *Famous Cases: Nine Trials that Changed the Law* (2002); and *Hanging in the Balance: A History of the Abolition of Capital Punishment in Britain* (1997) (with Brian P Block).

John Hostettler

Preface

This book is made up of short portrayals of a number of outstanding lawyers. Some of them are well-known not only for reasons of their work in the law but also for their activities in other fields. These include John Adams, Thomas Jefferson and Abraham Lincoln, all at different times President of the USA, and Marcus Tullius Cicero, arguably Rome's greatest lawyer and senator. A number of them were, or are, politicians; others were statesmen and, in one instance — William Howe and Abraham Hummel — they were sinister villains who were not only nefarious criminals but shameless with it. However, if being famous means being well-known for significant accomplishments Howe and Hummel certainly were famous.

In some cases, such as Henry Brougham, the Lord Chancellor of England who came within an ace of being Prime Minister, and Sir Edward Carson, known as the "Father of Northern Ireland", they combined law and politics in their rise to the top of both professions. In all cases mentioned here, where the law was not the primary interest of the person included, his or her legal training and background made a profound contribution to their success.

Some are not only famous but may be considered great whilst others, for various reasons, do not rise to that rank. For instance, I would include Lord Denning in the latter category although I am aware that such a view may well be challenged. He is extremely famous but can we regard as great a man who said he experienced no qualms about people being sentenced to death and was a retentionist who remarked on the utility of capital punishment years after it had been abolished? He also, in later life, strongly condemned people who were subsequently found to be innocent as well as being victims of serious miscarriages of justice.[1]

Clarence Darrow was a true humanist and undoubtedly the greatest lawyer in the history of the USA. He acted in defence of the underdog even when the underdogs were wealthy as with the sick murderers, Leopold and Loeb. It is astonishing how frequently he reduced juries, and even judges, to tears. His addresses to juries were often spread over several hours. They

---

1. See *Chapter 19*.

were direct and personal, and despite, or because of, that were generally persuasive and successful.

In earlier times Sir Edward Coke and Sir Matthew Hale both combined law and politics and have had a profound influence on the development of this country in the direction of democracy and human rights. Despite personal flaws, both had a deep understanding of, and faith in, the Common Law and the rudiments of the Rule of Law.

It will be noticed that only three women are included in the book. This is because there is no great history of women lawyers. Women were excluded from the legal profession until 1919 when, after their outstanding role in World War I, the ground-breaking Sex Disqualification (Removal) Act[2] of that year abolished all existing restrictions upon the admission of women into the professions. Section 1 of the Act deserves repeating. It stated that:

> A person shall not be disqualified by sex or marriage from the exercise of any public function, or from being appointed to or holding any civil or judicial office or post, or from entering or assuming or carrying on any civil profession or vocation, or for admission to any incorporated society (whether incorporated by Royal Charter or otherwise), and a person shall not be exempted by sex or marriage from the liability to serve as a juror.

Helena Kennedy QC, Gareth Peirce and Shami Chakrabarti, who appear here, are each significant civil liberties and human rights lawyers who have also, by their example, greatly enhanced the women's movement. Their careers show them to be true legal eagles.

Norman Birkett KC was regarded as the leading star at the criminal bar in the 1930s but to his regret he was not a great success as a judge, once outside the advocacy and the hurly-burly of criminal trials. James Fitzjames Stephen was a powerful voice in Victorian England but was too wedded to the importance of retribution in the law and coercion in politics to be a great man. Geoffrey Robertson is a modern human rights lawyer with many important legal successes to his name. He has a great sense of fun and this has brought him success in some rather bizarre cases.

---

2. 9 & 10 Geo. 5. c. 71.

Abraham Lincoln is better known for his abolition of slavery and pursuit of democracy in the USA than for his rather limited work as a lawyer but no one questions that he was a great man who believed in liberty and justice. Jeremy Bentham and Lord Brougham made significant contributions to the development of democracy in the United Kingdom and were steeped in the law whilst bringing about progressive change in other areas.

Sir Edward Marshall Hall was the last of our prominent actor-lawyers with his dramatic histrionics in the presence of juries — in the style of William Howe but without the criminality. Then, as society changed so the public and juries desired to see their lawyers talking instead of declaiming in the loudest possible voice and Marshall Hall's style went out of fashion.

In utter contrast to Marshall Hall stands Gareth Peirce a human rights solicitor who shuns publicity but whose name has virtually passed into folklore for her tenacious defences of alleged bombers, terrorists and members of minority groups.

Finally, there is Cesare Beccaria, a great man whose influence in making criminal law in many countries more humane is incalculable. He believed that,

> In order that every punishment may not be an act of violence, committed by one man or by many against a single individual, it ought to be above all things public, speedy, necessary, the least possible in the given circumstances, proportioned to its crime [and] dictated by the laws.

That message he sent successfully across a Europe riven with secret trials and torture. And, like Beccaria, all the lawyers included here have had a profound effect in their various ways on the lives of others.

Where possible I have included references to key cases as well as turning points and major contributions to legal history in order to provide a thread involving disparate types of men and women in different periods of history and differing cultures. Instead of placing my choice of famous lawyers in alphabetical order I have chosen my own order to mix them up a little and start and end with those I think most suitable in giving a sense of variety. Of course, the reader may pick and choose as he or she wishes.

Some famous lawyers, including Sir William Garrow and Thomas (Lord) Erskine are not included because I have written about them at some length in the recent past. Garrow, in Old Bailey trials, revolutionised the criminal law and was largely responsible for the introduction of adversary trial and human rights for prisoners. Erskine shone in a number of state trials that rocked England and helped keep at bay a virtual reign of terror by a government that feared the spread to this country of the effects of The Terror of the French Revolution and, but for Erskine, very nearly brought it about themselves.[3] Garrow in particular had an important influence on the future of the criminal law and the Constitution of this country as well as having a substantial effect upon adversary trial and the Rule of Law in other lands.

Others are missing because there are so many famous lawyers, since the law impinges on all our lives, so that it is impossible to include a great many of them in a book of this kind. Their sheer numbers, however, are a tribute to trial by jury, adversary trial and the Rule of Law. Countries that use the inquisitorial system of trial have far fewer lawyers in proportion to their populations since there is no need for them in a system which limits their role in and out of the courtroom.

Restorative justice which has advanced considerably in the last two decades has an important role to play in its approach to harm, problem-solving and violations of legal and human rights. It can involve meetings of the parties and others to discuss the crime and its effects, to give offenders an opportunity to repair the harm they have caused and restore both victims and offenders to being contributing members of the community. But restorative justice measures are in the United Kingdom introduced within the framework of the adversarial system of trial and should not be seen, as some of its more enthusiastic supporters suggest, as an alternative to it. Rather, they are possible because of the security and strengths of adversary trial.

Adversary trial defends the integrity of an accused person, *inter alia*, by the presumption of innocence, access to counsel, exclusionary rules of evidence and the right to cross-examine. Alongside trial by jury, which like adversary trial, is under attack from some prominent politicians, it ensures

---

3. For more information about these two 'famous lawyers', see John Hostettler and Richard Braby (2010), *Sir William Garrow: His Life, Times and Fight for Justice;* and John Hostettler (2010), *Thomas Erskine and Trial by Jury*. Both Sherfield-on-Loddon: Waterside Press.

that prisoners are protected from state authoritarianism and enables citizens to take a stand against the power of the state and vested interests. As a consequence, the skills and integrity of our trial lawyers honed in forensic battle are formidable.

I trust the reader will enjoy the brief lives of those I have chosen to appear in this book.

Twenty Famous Lawyers

Chapter 1

Clarence Darrow

Freedom and Humanity

Clarence Darrow stands out as one of the greatest lawyers in the history of the USA. Admitted to the Ohio bar in 1878, he was fearless and outspoken as a defence advocate. Loved or bitterly hated by most of his American contemporaries, his name became a legend while he was still alive and was battling his way through the courts. He could be quixotic, sceptical, even a showman. But above all he was passionate in his belief in justice for all and his loathing of bigotry, hate and ignorance. He represented both the poor and the rich, but was always on the side of the underdog who could, as with Leopold and Loeb (see later in this chapter), be members of wealthy families. His empathy with and power over juries was extraordinary. With his lowly, simple and down-to-earth approach he seemed to reach into the very minds of those sitting in the jury box. And although he made many enemies with his satiric and biting attacks on prosecutors, he could move a judge and jurors to tears at the end of a plea for a prisoner whose very life hung by the proverbial thread.

Darrow's enemies constantly looked for his self-destruction. But although he sometimes seemed to go too far, they waited in vain. Even when they prosecuted him on a trumped-up charge of attempting to bribe a witness in a trade union trial he secured a triumphant acquittal—with the jurors weeping and the spectators going wild with joy.[1] Despite prejudice from employers, judges and politicians alike, Darrow triumphed through the combination

---
1. 15 May 1912. The trial arose from the *McNamara Case* in Los Angeles.

of his brilliance, his humanity, his belief in liberty and his determination to help any accused person who was not likely to get a fair trial — usually the active trade unionist, the black man or woman and the Communist.

Many such people owed their lives, and many more their liberty, to Clarence Darrow. How did he do it? How could he win so often in the America of the early-20th-century with its widespread racial hatred and lynchings, with the armed and violent Pinkerton detectives and the use of gangsters to shoot down trade unionists on strike?

Charge of Criminal Conspiracy

Take the trial of Thomas I. Kidd for example. Kidd was a trade union organizer and general-secretary of the Amalgamated Woodworkers' International Union. The case arose from a strike in the factory of George M. Paine in Winsconsin at a time when trade unions in the USA were portrayed by the press as criminal conspiracies.

As a picket in a strike lasting 14 weeks, Kidd was charged, in 1898, along with two other union men, with criminal conspiracy to injure the business of Paine's Lumber Company. The prosecution was represented by the district attorney and F. W. Houghton, a special counsel appointed to assist the attorney. Darrow, himself the son of a woodworker, acted for the defendants and decided to show that it was Paine and not the state of Wisconsin that was the actual complainant in the case. He was assisted in this when in court Houghton rushed to the industrialist's side, fawningly led him to the lawyers' table and shook his hand warmly before putting him on the witness stand. Darrow commented to the jury later,

> Houghton would have been glad to lick the dust from Paine's boots had he been given the opportunity to perform the service.[2]

Darrow told the jury that, whatever it was in form, this was not really a criminal case. "It was", he argued,

---

2. Clarence Darrow. Verbatim Speeches in *Clarence Darrow: Attorney for the Damned* (1957), (ed. Arthur Weinberg), London: Macdonald. p. 268.

but an episode in the great battle for human liberty, a battle which was commenced when the tyranny and oppression of man first caused him to impose upon his fellows and which will not end so long as the children of one father shall be compelled to toil to support the children of another in luxury and ease.

He then set out to reveal to the jury—and the world—the slave-like conditions of the workers in George M. Paine's factory. Fines and other penalties could be imposed if a worker broke one of Paine's rules. One rule stated that, "No unnecessary talking will be allowed during working hours". A clear breach of the US Constitution remarked Darrow, keeping a straight face. Another rule was that, "Loud talking or shouting in or around the mill and factory cannot be allowed except in case of accident or fire". Darrow told the jury,

> I suppose the old gentleman is nervous; and if he is, they ought not to talk loud. It is very kind of him to let them shout when there is a fire. Some men would not do it; but George M. Paine is good, and so if there is a fire they can shout, or if anyone gets hurt, they can talk loud. It is a beautiful institution.[3]

He lashed out at the infamy that kept workers locked in the factory by armed guards from 6.45 am until night. And he showed that it was through the labour and toil of these imprisoned men that Paine had grown rich and prosperous. Brilliantly describing the struggles of the trade unionists and the unacceptable practices of the employer he addressed the jury for two days and wrung from them a verdict of not guilty. A remarkable achievement at a time of deeply disturbed labour relations in the country.

The Communist Trial

In Chicago in 1920, 20 Communists were arrested and charged with advocating the overthrow of the government by force. The background to the case was the unprecedented raids of the xenophobic USA Attorney-General, A. Mitchell Palmer. These were known as the "Palmer Raids" which he said would "sweep the nation clean of such alien filth". "The sharp tongue of

---

3. *Ibid.* p. 280.

the Revolution's head", he roundly declared, "was licking the alters of the churches, leaping into the belfry of the school bell, crawling into the scared corners of American homes and seeking to replace marriage vows with libertine laws". In the raids 6,000 radicals were rounded up on New Year's Day 1920, many of whom were imprisoned whilst others were deported.

The trial was heard in the Criminal Court of Chicago with Judge Oscar Hebel presiding. Darrow acted for the defence. One of the defendant's was William Lloyd who, it was shown, had driven down State Street in Chicago with both an American and a red flag flying from his car. Later he told a Socialist meeting in Milwaukee,

> What we want is preparedness. We want to organize so that if you want every Socialist in Milwaukee at a certain place at a certain time, with a rifle or a bad egg in his hand, he will be there.

In his closing remarks, Attorney Barnhart for the state said to the jury, "He had the red flag tied over the American flag to show his contempt for Old Glory. Think of it, gentlemen, this defendant indicating his contempt for the government by displaying the red flag of the revolution".

When it came to Darrow's turn to address the jury he told them:

> Now, gentlemen, let me be plain about it. If you want to convict these 20 men, then do it. If you have any idea in your heads that I want you to protect them or save them, forget it. They are no better than any other 20 men; they are no better than the millions and tens of millions down through the ages who have been prosecuted—yes, and convicted, in cases like this; and if it is necessary for my clients, gentlemen, to show that America is like all the rest, if it is necessary that my clients shall go to prison to show it, then let them go. They can afford it if you gentlemen can; make no mistake about that.

He told the jury that what interested him was whether they would do something in the cause of freedom of speech and the principles for which men had shed their blood in every age and every land. He would not argue whether the defendants' ideas were right or wrong. He was not bound to believe them right in order to take their case and the jurors were not bound to believe them right in order to find them not guilty. But the humblest and meanest man who lives, even the idlest and silliest, man who lives, should have his say. Yet policemen had twice violated the Constitution. They had entered his clients' homes without a search warrant and seized property and overhauled their papers. From beginning to end the case had been marked by the most flagrant violations of the law and every effort to magnify, to create passion and prejudice to persuade the jury to deny freedom of speech. And the red flag was the flag of the first colonists in the USA and of the common people throughout history.

Darrow made a lengthy and impassioned speech for the rights of all men and women to freedom of speech and dealt with all the evidence which had been given for the prosecution. The trial lasted for ten weeks and at the end Darrow told the jury, "You can only protect your liberties in this world by protecting the other man's freedom. You can only be free if I am free". He asked the jury to do its part in the "great cause of human freedom, for which men have ever fought and died".

The jury retired for only a few hours and in the climate of fear and hysteria of the time it was inevitable that they would find the defendants guilty. They were sentenced to imprisonment ranging from one to five years and fines. An appeal to the Illinois Supreme Court failed but Chief Justice Orrin Carter gave a vigorous dissenting judgment in favour of open and free discussion of all public questions about the necessity of changing laws and the form of government. On the basis of this judgment, the Governor of Illinois, Len Small, on 29 November 1922 pardoned 16 of the defendants before they had served a day of their sentence. The others had emigrated or died before the pardon was announced.[4]

Leopold and Loeb

Throughout his life Darrow was opposed to capital punishment and in over 100 murder trials incredibly he lost only one. Despite his normal rumpled appearance in court he had a brilliant mind and could move juries and judges to tears with his eloquence. He is best known for his defence in the summer of 1924 of Nathan Leopold and Richard Loeb the sons of two wealthy

---

4. Arthur Weinberg (ed.) (1957), *Clarence Darrow: Attorney for the Damned, Op. cit.* p. 173.

Chicago families. At the time Leopold was 19 and Loeb was 18. Leopold was a law student about to enter Harvard Law School and his father was a retired millionaire box manufacturer. Loeb was the youngest graduate ever from the University of Michigan whilst his father was the multi-millionaire vice-president of the prestigious Sears, Roebuck Company.

The boys had been raised in great wealth and luxury since childhood. After they were arrested they were charged with the murder of Bobby Franks, a 14-year-old boy. Without hesitation they confessed to the crime. Their motive for the murder, they claimed, was a pure love of excitement. This was to be the "Trial of the Century" blazoned the Chicago newspapers. In utter despair the parents of the boys, who could have afforded to engage any counsel in the USA pleaded with Darrow to represent their sons and he agreed to do so.

Darrow had the youths plead guilty in order to avoid the trial being held before a jury that might be pitiless in the frantic atmosphere surrounding the trial. In any event, in addition to the confessions, near to where the victim's body was found were also found Leopold's spectacles with traceable frames. In court, Darrow contended that it was not a conscious choice between right and wrong[5] that determined human behaviour but powerful psychological, physical and environmental influences. Before a judge alone, Darrow argued that the prisoners were mentally diseased. This was not special pleading by counsel. In fact, both boys had severe mental illnesses. Leopold was a schizophrenic who had fallen in love with Loeb whom he saw as a superman. Loeb cynically agreed to enter into a homosexual relationship with Leopold on condition that Leopold would agree to a crime relationship and kill as an experiment to commit the perfect crime. Loeb actually planned and executed the murder but with the full support of Leopold.[6]

Darrow in shirtsleeves, and with braces held by his thumbs, dominated the courtroom and his closing address lasted for 12 hours over three days with people storming the courtroom to hear him. He stressed that there had never been a case in Chicago where youths who were minors (at the time this meant under 21-years-of-age) who pleaded guilty had been sentenced to death. He put on the witness stand psychiatrists to prove that the boys were mentally diseased and he pleaded for mercy. The only way to soften

---

5. The basis of the M'Naughten Rules in murder trials in England.
6. Irving Stone. (1949) *Darrow for the Defence*. London, The Bodley Head. pp. 378, 341.

the human heart, he said, was through charity, love and understanding. He begged the judge not to turn back to a barbarous and cruel past. He declared,

> You may stand them up on the trap door of the scaffold, and choke them to death, but that act will be infinitely more cold-blooded, whether justified or not, than any act that these boys have committed or can commit.

In the event Darrow succeeded and the boys were not sentenced to death. However Judge Caverly sentenced them to life imprisonment, and, in the USA manner, added a further 99 years. Whilst in prison Loeb was killed by a fellow prisoner and Leopold went on to set up an educational system for prisoners.

During the trial Darrow was accused in the press of greed in presenting a million-dollar defence for two wealthy families. As a consequence he got the families, who had desperately pleaded with him to defend their children, to issue a public statement that he would not be paid heavy legal fees and that his fees would be calculated by officers from the Chicago Bar Association. Darrow thought $200,000 would be reasonable since the trial had lasted more than four weeks but after lengthy negotiations with the families, who proved to be the greedy ones, he received only gross fees of $70,000 which after deducting expenses and taxes left him with $30,000.

The Monkey Trial

In 1925, Tennessee was the scene of the famous "Monkey Trial" when a 24-year-old high school teacher was prosecuted for explaining the meaning of evolution to his class. The newspapers dubbed it "America's most amazing trial". On 21 March 1925 a statute known as the Butler Act had been passed by the Tennessee state legislature. This forbade the teaching in any state-funded school in Tennessee of any theory that denied the story of the divine creation of man as presented in the *Bible* or to teach that man was descended from a lower order of animals. Evolution of any species of animal or plant was in order but to teach the evolution of mankind was illegal. Many other states were preparing to follow with their own anti-evolution laws. Science teaching in schools was likely to be outlawed.

Thomas Scopes decided to test this law in the courts and discussed evolution in his class. As a consequence William Jennings Bryan, leader of the Fundamentalist Movement and former candidate for President of the USA, decided to head the prosecution of Scopes in what became the Scopes Evolution Case in Dayton, Tennessee. Darrow, now approaching 70-years-of-age agreed to defend Scopes without fee and, indeed, at the end of the trial he was some $2,000 out of pocket. All America seemed to head for Dayton in July to witness this battle of forensic giants. What had been a quiet backwater soon resembled Coney Island and a circus with crowds of Fundamentalists, Anarchists, Holy Rollers, Free-thinkers, newspaper and media people. To this was added some scores of kiosks to supply them with food and drink. The town was filled with signs which read,

"You need God in your Business",

"Sweethearts, Come to Jesus"; and

"Where Will You Spend Eternity?"

Many shops had comic posters in their windows depicting monkeys and coconuts. Sections of the press referred to the "Ape Trial". And Bryan had offered a hundred dollars in cash to any university professor who would sign an affidavit saying that he was personally descended from an ape.

Darrow told the court that the *Bible* was not one book but 66 books written over a period of 1,000 years. It dealt with religion and morals not science. He gave examples of which space allows only a few to be mentioned here. It was not a book on geology, he said, those who wrote it knew nothing about geology. It was not a book on biology, they knew nothing about it. It was not a work on astronomy, those who studied the heavens at the time believed the earth was the centre of the universe. Yet this law made a teacher who taught evolution a criminal.

Darrow endeavoured to put in the witness box scientists to give expert evidence in the case but the judge refused to let them testify. On the other hand, he agreed to let Bryan give evidence as a self-proclaimed expert on the *Bible*. Under Darrow's cross-examination, Bryan said that everything in it should be believed. He accepted that the whale swallowed Jonah and that Joshua made the sun stand still. He affirmed that the Flood occurred in the year 2348 BC and the world was exactly 4,004-years-old. Eve was the first woman and was literally made out of Adam's rib; the sun was made on the fourth day and so on. Bryan made such a fool of himself that the judge, who was sympathetic to him, refused to allow further questioning and incredibly had Bryan's testimony, given over a whole day, struck from the record.

Not surprisingly, however, Scopes was found guilty and was fined $100. The verdict was reversed by the Tennessee Supreme Court a year later on a technicality. A few days after the trial, Bryan died. But Darrow had made an international plea against oppression, bigotry and ignorance. The trial was turned into a play called 'Inherit the Wind', which was adapted as a popular film with Spencer Tracey portraying Darrow.

A Racial Hatred Case
This trial was heard in the city of Detroit in 1926. During the First World War the motor industry in Detroit was in the midst of a boom and black workers were brought there from the South to work in the booming factories. However, no provision was made for housing them and some moved into so-called white districts.

Dr. Ossian Sweet was black but he was not an automobile worker. He was a successful gynaecologist who had worked under Madame Curie on the effects of radium on cancer. He returned to his home town of Detroit from Europe and when he looked for a home for himself, his wife and their two-year-old baby girl he could find one only and that was in a lower middle-class white neighbourhood. The family moved in and two days later a crowd of several hundred whites besieged the house. Windows were smashed and the mob surged forward with shouts of, "Here's niggers. Get them! Get them"!

A gunshot rang out from the house which killed one of the white men. Dr. Sweet and ten black friends who were in the house were arrested and charged with first degree murder. Darrow was appointed chief defence counsel in the case and the trial of the eleven defendants began on 30 October 1925 before an all-white jury. The defence was self-defence in an anti-black riot situation.

The prosecution contended that there was no mob around the Sweet home when the man was killed and prosecution witnesses testified that they were near to it only out of curiosity. Nonetheless, Darrow established in cross-examination that on the Sweet's moving-in an association had been formed to keep out black people from the district. And on asking one witness how many people were outside the house he replied, "There was a great crowd—no, I won't say a great crowd, a large crowd—well, there were a few people and the officers were keeping them moving". Darrow swooped and asked if the witness had talked with anyone about the case? Yes, replied the witness, with Lieutenant Johnson.

"And when you started to answer the question you forgot to say 'a few people' didn't you"?

"Yes, sir", came the reply that changed the nature of the case.[7]

After a retirement of 46 hours the jury was unable to agree and the judge declared a mistrial. Thereafter the defendants were to be tried separately.

Some five months later, in April 1926, Henry Sweet, a 21-year-old student and younger brother of Dr. Sweet, was tried for the same offence in a test case and Darrow's final speech to the jury lasted for seven hours. He said that although the prosecution had argued that race and colour had nothing to do with the case, there was nothing but prejudice in it. "If it was reversed and eleven white men had shot and killed a black while protecting their home and their lives against a mob of blacks" they would not have been indicted, they would have been given medals instead. He then told the all-white jury that each of them was prejudiced against black people and he wanted them to guard against it. Probably not one of them, he said, had visited a black person in his home or had invited a black person to dinner. Yet they knew, if only from the witnesses in the case, that there were "coloured people living right here in the city of Detroit [who] are intellectually the equals and some of them superior to most of us".

He then established that the man who was shot was a member of the mob and had enticed the crowd to violence and stone-throwing that broke the windows of the house. And he concluded with these words:

> This case is about to end, gentlemen. To them, it is life. Not one of their color sits on this jury. Their fate is in the hands of 12 whites. Their eyes are fixed on you, their hearts go out to you, and their hopes hang on your verdict.
>
> This is all. I ask you, on behalf of this defendant, on behalf of these helpless ones who turn to you, and more than that—on behalf of this great state, and this great

---

7. *Clarence Darrow: Attorney for the Damned. Op. cit.* (ed. Arthur Weinberg). pp. 231-2.

city which must face this problem, and face it fairly—I ask you, in the name of progress and of the human race, to return a verdict of Not Guilty in this case![8]

It is a tribute to Darrow's greatness that on the following day the jury returned a verdict of not guilty and none of the other cases came to trial. The Sweet family never moved back into the house but today both whites and blacks live in the neighbourhood. Darrow's closing speech is today seen as a landmark in the Civil Rights Movement and was included in the book, *Speeches that Changed the World* under the heading, "I Believe in the Law of Love".

Darrow died on 13 March 1938, aged 80, and his exploits and his humanity have become part of the fabric of the history of the USA.

---

8. *Ibid.* p. 263.

Twenty Famous Lawyers

Chapter 2

Edward Carson
Strong Man of Politics and the Law

Edward Carson (later Sir Edward) was born in Dublin, then part of the United Kingdom, on 9 February 1854. He is best known for his political career, culminating in his appointment by Lloyd George as First Lord of the Admiralty in the First World War, and as the "Uncrowned King of Ulster". Nevertheless, in his day he was a famous lawyer, an intrepid advocate both in Ireland and in England, and the finest orator of the time.[1]

"Coercion Carson"

After graduating at Trinity College, Dublin Carson was called to the Irish Bar in the Easter Term of 1877 and began to practise, although without much initial success. His chance came ten years later, however, with his appointment as junior counsel to the Attorney-General to assist in enforcing the draconian Crimes Act[2] of that year. The Act gave new power to the Lord Lieutenant of Ireland to declare any association dangerous and illegal and it was directed primarily against the Land League which supported tenants fighting their landlords. It also gave the authorities power to remove criminal trials from their locality and bring them before special juries—property holders selected by the Crown—instead of common juries. So-called serious offences, such as conspiracy and unlawful assembly, were to be tried without

---

1. For a biography of Carson see John Hostettler. (1997), *Sir Edward Carson: A Dream Too Far.* Chichester, Barry Rose Law Publishers.
2. Criminal Law and Procedure (Ireland) Act, 1887.

any jury at all and witnesses were compelled to give evidence even if it might incriminate them. No less than 5,000 men and women were charged under the Act in three years and Carson became known as "Coercion Carson".

"Fed on Vinegar"

In appearance, at the time, Carson was described by William O'Brien MP as a liverish looking young man, "with the complexion of one fed on vinegar and with features as inexpressive as a jagged hatchet". In fact, Carson's striking appearance was often of great assistance to him in court. Tall and lean with a hatchet-shaped face and scornful eyes that seemed to bore through a witness he rattled many an opponent merely by looking at them. Of more importance, however, was that, although when prosecuting he was likened to a fighter wielding a shillelagh or bludgeon rather than a rapier, he was also assisted by an intuitive sense of what was going on in a person's mind. His cross-examinations were often devastating. His pugnacity served him well in court and he was sufficiently successful that at the age of 35 he took silk and became the youngest QC in Ireland.

A Battered Skull

One of his first cases as a silk was the trial of Father McFadden and others in 1888 on charges of murder and conspiracy. Father McFadden was the parish priest of the barren and far-flung district of Gweedore in County Donegal. He was a resolute and militant man who had already served a term of imprisonment for urging his parishioners to work for the Plan of Campaign which aimed to persuade tenants to withhold their rents from tyrannical landlords. The police endeavoured to serve a warrant of re-arrest under the Crimes Act when he was leaving his church after saying Mass. As a consequence, the congregation charged at the seven policemen involved and knocked them down. Their superior officer, Inspector Martin, then drew his sword whereupon the crowd turned upon him and battered in his skull.

Twenty-three men were subsequently arrested, of whom ten were charged with murder and 13 with conspiracy. At the trial Carson was one of the prosecutors. The prisoner who had first struck the inspector was found guilty of manslaughter and sentenced to ten years' penal servitude. With the others, the jury disagreed since the inspector had drawn his sword, and counsel on both sides agreed to proceed on lesser charges. All the remaining prisoners then pleaded guilty and some received relatively light sentences including Father McFadden, who was bound over for obstructing the police. The subsequent release by chief secretary Morley of those who were imprisoned caused bitter party controversy at Westminster.

Trial for Murder

Carson was strongly opposed to capital punishment and this was clearly expressed when he defended men charged with murder. One such case arose when on 28 March 1882 three friends, Joseph MacMahon, John Brennan and Thomas Martin entered a public house in Dorset Street, Dublin and requested a private room. Five minutes after they were shown to a room a shot rang out and Brennan emerged from the room and ran off. He was pursued by a crowd and eventually pulled off a jaunting car. Martin had remained with the dead body of MacMahon and two revolvers were found on the floor of the room, one fully-loaded and the other with one bullet fired.

Carson took on the defence of the prisoners in a highly charged atmosphere not helped by the discovery of an arsenal of weapons in MacMahon's home. Violence had reached serious proportions in Dublin and only a few weeks later Lord Frederick Cavendish, the Irish Chief Secretary, and the under-secretary Thomas Burke were slashed to death with 12-inch-long surgical knives in Phoenix Park in broad daylight.

In the trial of Brennan and Martin before the respected Chief Baron Palles, Carson put it to the jury that the homicide was an accident and called as a witness for the defence the driver of the jaunting car who testified that Brennan had told him to drive back to the public house to help a dying man. On the other hand, the Crown prosecutor made much of the "alarming state of affairs prevailing in the city". Carson, however, urged the jury not to convict on a capital charge because of the disturbed state of the city. There was, he said, no motive for murder. Moreover, the public house had been crowded, it was broad daylight and two police officers were in the street outside. "Is it likely", he asked, "if a murder was intended, the murderer would use a weapon which must bring upon him immediate detection"? He concluded, "I do not ask for mercy: I demand justice".[3]

The jury were unable to agree upon a verdict and the prisoners were remanded for a re-trial. This time they entered pleas of manslaughter which were accepted by the Crown and they were sentenced to terms of imprisonment. Mr Justice Lawton, who presided over the second trial, was himself shot at in the street and thereafter always sat in court with a loaded revolver on the Bench.

Following a further series of high-profile trials the Chief Secretary for Ireland desired to have Carson in the House of Commons to act as an English law officer and an opponent of the powerful Irish Nationalist MPs. Accordingly as a Liberal-Unionist he was elected as one of the Members for Trinity College and his political future was determined. His duty, he explained, was to preserve "intact the union between Great Britain and Ireland". At the same time he arranged to be called to the English Bar and joined the chambers of Charles Darling, QC, MP at No.3 Dr Johnson's Buildings in The Temple.

W S Gilbert

One of Carson's early cases in England involved W S Gilbert. Gilbert of "Gilbert and Sullivan" fame, who bitterly caricatured Oscar Wilde in the comic opera "Patience", but who was himself sensitive to criticism. He had written an unsuccessful play called "The Fortune Hunter" during the production of which in Edinburgh he gave an interview to a Scottish newspaper. In it he attacked the professional ability of several prominent actors whom he named, including Sir Herbert Tree and Sir Henry Irving, who, he claimed, could not make a speech "at all interesting". Many actors were furious and, in response, Irving made an angry attack on Gilbert.

An article then appeared in the widely-read theatrical journal *Era* accusing Gilbert of unbearable conceit and ingratitude to the artists who had made his fortune. "Mr Gilbert's self-esteem," it continued,

> has with advancing years developed into a malady. In his own estimation he is a kind of Grand Llama or Sacred Elephant of dramatic literature ... That Grundy

---

3. H. Montgomery Hyde. (1953) *Carson. The Life of Sir Edward Carson, Lord Carson of Duncairn.* London, Hamish Hamilton. p. 39.

[another well-known playwright] should have written successful original works, while he, the Great Gilbert, has met with failure after failure in modern drama, is preposterous and not to be borne.

Gilbert, though a barrister himself and aware of the risks, sued for libel. He briefed Lawson Walton QC and Edward Marshall Hall (*Chapter 17*), whilst Carson appeared for the *Era*. The article, the defence pleaded, was fair comment on a matter of public interest. In the course of cross-examination by Carson, Gilbert would not allow of his well-known rift with Sir Arthur Sullivan, but he did admit to bitter feuds with their impresario Richard D'Oyly Carte. He also confessed to ending a lifelong friendship with Clement Scott for criticising one of his plays.

In reply to one question he said, "I did say that it was no longer necessary for me to be a cockshy for a lot of low class critics". He admitted "The Fortune Hunter" was "a very bad play" but wanted no one else to say so. Even favourable criticisms did not please him. "I never read favourable criticisms", he said, and added, "I prefer reading unfavourable ones. I know how good I am, but I do not know how bad I am".

Carson then quoted a piece from Gilbert's own "Rosencratz and Guildenstern":

> The acts were five — though by five acts too long,
> I wrote an act by way of epilogue,
> An act by which the penalty of death
> Was meted out to all who sneered at it.
> The play was not good, but the punishment
> Of those who laughed at it was capital.

"Those were the words of Claudius of Denmark," Gilbert retorted, "not of myself". "I leave it to the jury," observed Carson, "whether you did not repeat King Claudius's words in the box a moment ago". When, towards the end of the case, Carson was addressing the jury Gilbert walked out of the court in a huff.

The judge summed up against Gilbert but the jury, among whom were no doubt some Gilbert and Sullivan comic opera fans, proved unable to agree.

Gilbert never forgave Carson. Even years later, at dinner parties, he would turn his back and refuse to speak to him.

Oscar Wilde

After various further successes in English courts Carson became involved in the case of Oscar Wilde. By 1891, Wilde's triumphant success was acclaimed with two of his plays running concurrently to crowded theatres in London. But this was also the year in which he met Lord Alfred Douglas, the son of the Marquess of Queensberry who is remembered for the Queensbury Rules of Boxing which were named after him. The Marquess firmly believed that his son had been seduced into a gay relationship by Wilde. A violent husband, a callous father and a coarse-minded brute who was undoubtedly mentally-unbalanced, he decided to bring matters to a head and left a visiting card for Wilde at the Albermarle Club. On the back of it he had written "To Oscar Wilde posing as a somdomite" (sic). Wilde, against his better judgment, was persuaded by Lord Alfred to institute a private prosecution against Queensberry for criminal libel. Because he had had a slight acquaintance with Wilde in Ireland Carson was reluctant to appear against him but he overcame his scruples and accepted instructions to lead for the defence.

The trial commenced at the Old Bailey on 3 April 1895 before Mr Justice Henn Collins and a jury. Wilde gave his evidence briefly. But under Carson's cross-examination he made the foolish mistake of showing off and answering back. This scored some points but Carson persisted and waited quietly for Wilde to fall into a trap.

Quoting from Wilde's novel, *The Picture of Dorian Gray*, Carson asked, "Have you ever adored a young man madly"? Wilde replied, "I have never given adoration to anybody except myself" (Much laughter).

In reply to other questions he said, "Everything I write is extraordinary" and "I rarely think anything I write is true". Then came the turning point. Wilde was asked about a young boy named Grainger who was Lord Alfred's servant at Oxford.

"Did you kiss him?" asked Carson, his flashing eyes mesmerising the witness.

"Oh dear no," replied Wilde off his guard. "He was a peculiarly plain boy. He was unfortunately extremely ugly. I pitied him for it".

The damage was done. Carson pounced like a tiger. Why, why, he persisted had he mentioned the boy's ugliness? Wilde was finished. After further pitiless cross-examination the jury found the Marquess not guilty. As had occurred before, Carson won the case solely by cross-examination and without calling any witnesses for the defence.[4]

Wilde was then arrested and prosecuted for homosexual offences under a newly-enacted criminal law, despite Carson suggesting that the case be dropped since Wilde had suffered a great deal. Wilde was found guilty and, with unseemly public jubilation, sentenced to two years hard labour which he served mainly in Reading Gaol where he also wrote *De Profundis* a tragic and disturbing letter to Lord Alfred. On his release he went to France where he died three years later a broken and impoverished wreck of a man. Fortunately his literary works and his fame live on.[5]

Cadbury Anguish

Just prior to the January 1910 general election, Carson appeared for seven days in a case on the Midland Circuit that involved issues of politics, the press, law, morality and big business. The action was one of libel against Standard Newspapers, a Conservative group which controlled the *Standard,* the *Evening Standard* and the *St. James's Gazette.* The plaintiffs were Cadburys, the well-known chocolate manufacturers who were prominent Quakers, temperance reformers and philanthropists. Their reputation was also high for caring for the social welfare of their employees.

During the 1906 general election campaign the Cadburys' newspaper, the Liberal *Daily News* had denounced the Balfour government for allowing the importation into colonial South Africa of tens of thousands of Chinese indentured workers for employment underground as slave labourers in the diamond mines. Pictures of such workers in chains and subjected to flogging were displayed with the argument that the government wanted them rather than have whites working with blacks. In response, other newspapers retorted that a good deal of raw material used by Cadburys in its chocolates and cocoa was itself the product of slave labour in Portuguese tropical islands off the coast of West Africa, at which they connived. Cadburys

---
4. *Ibid.* pp.70-79.
5. Not least Wilde's epic poem, *The Ballad of Reading Gaol.*

commissioned an inquiry as a result of which they ceased buying raw cocoa from the islands in January 1909.

In the meantime, on 26 September 1908 the *Standard* newspaper wrote about the "monstrous trade in human flesh and blood" and slave-driving and slave-dealing that fed the mills and presses of their factory at Bournville, near Birmingham. Cadburys issued a writ for libel and if they believed they would come out of it with clean hands they clearly miscalculated and underestimated Carson. The case commenced at Birmingham Assizes before Mr Justice Pickford and a special jury on 29 November 1909. Rufus Isaacs KC and John Simon KC led for the plaintiffs and Sir Edward Carson KC and Eldon Bankes KC for the defendants.

Isaacs outlined what good employers the plaintiffs were and how they had endeavoured to alleviate conditions in the Portuguese islands. After William Cadbury had given evidence, there was cheering in court and all seemed set fair for the plaintiffs' victory. But now it was Carson's turn to subject the witness to one of the most blistering cross-examinations of his career. He first established that Cadburys had for years bought raw material from planters who to their knowledge had used slave labour.

> *Carson:* The cocoa you were buying was procured by atrocious methods of slavery?
> *Cadbury:* Yes.
> *Carson:* Men, women and children taken forcibly away from their homes against their will?
> *Cadbury:* Yes.
> *Carson:* From the information which you procured, did they go down in shackles?
> *Cadbury:* It is the usual custom, I believe, to shackle them at night on the march.
> *Carson:* Those who could not keep up with the march were murdered?
> *Cadbury:* I have seen statements to that effect.
> *Carson:* You do not doubt it?
> *Cadbury:* I do not doubt that it has been so in some cases.
> *Carson:* The children born to the women who are taken out as slaves become the property of the owners of the slaves?
> *Cadbury:* I believe that the children born on the estate do. I have never been able to find any regulation that gives a child any freedom.

> *Carson:* Knowing it was atrocious, you took the main portion of your supply of cocoa for the profit of your business from the islands conducted under this system?
> *Cadbury:* Yes, for a period of some years.
> *Carson:* You do not look on that as anything immoral?
> *Cadbury:* Not under the circumstances.

The cross-examination continued relentlessly and finally ended with a question which considerably upset the witness.

> *Carson:* Have you formed any estimate of the number of slaves who lost their lives in preparing your cocoa during those eight years?
> *Cadbury:* (Clearly agitated) No, no, no.

As he commonly did, Carson relied solely upon the effect of his cross-examination. He called no witnesses for the defence. In addressing the jury he stressed that, although the plaintiffs had argued to the contrary, race was the one vital issue in the case. Isaacs complained that the defence had "relied on a speech of singular power and scorn and invective by Sir Edward Carson". At the end of his address to the jury, Isaacs once more received loud applause. The judge then summed up strongly in favour of Cadburys saying that unless the jury believed they had acted dishonestly and had not done what they said they had done to mitigate conditions on the islands they were entitled to succeed. The newspaper's attack was not fair comment but a serious charge against the honesty of character of the plaintiffs.

It is curious how Cadburys were able to admit their products were produced by slavery whilst claiming to be champions of morality. But contrary to the views of Isaacs, the judge and spectators in the courtroom Carson's instinct about the reaction of the jury in the face of the evidence proved correct. They found for the plaintiffs on the law but awarded them damages of one farthing—a clear moral victory for Carson and his clients.

Cadbury's have, of course, been famous for their philanthropic role over nearly 200 years. The first Cadbury shop was opened in Birmingham by John Cadbury in 1824. Bourneville, called "The Factory in a Garden", was built in 1879 with the direct intent of providing congenial conditions and healthy opportunities for its workforce. The company's philanthropic reputation suffered severely from the exposures and admissions in the trial. It subsequently managed to redeem itself to an extent and on 2 February 2010 Cadbury's became part of Kraft Foods who undertook to continue the company's philanthropic traditions. The takeover was only a little more than three years ago, however, and the jury is still out on what the consequences will be.

The Archer-Shee Case
At the age of 13 years George Archer-Shee, a cadet at the Royal Naval College at Osborne on the Isle of Wight, was accused of the theft of a postal order from a fellow cadet. It might appear to have been a trifling matter but for Carson it involved the young man's honour in a David and Goliath battle in which the whole weight of the Admiralty was brought to bear on the boy. And, in the event, the spleen of the Liberal government was to be levelled at Carson.

The case against the boy seemed watertight. On 7 October 1908 a fellow cadet, Terence Back, had received a postal order for five shillings. That afternoon Archer-Shee had obtained permission to go to the nearby post office to buy a postal order to enable him to purchase a model train which cost 15 shillings and sixpence.[6] When he got back to the college it had been reported that Back's postal order had been stolen. Miss Tucker, in charge of the post office, was called and she stated that only two cadets had visited that afternoon and the same cadet who had bought a postal order for 15 shillings and sixpence had also cashed the five shillings order. George declared that this was quite untrue.

Carson, whose own son Walter had only recently left the college, accepted the brief to appear for the boy after questioning him for three hours to establish that he was telling the truth. By a quirk of fate it was Carson who later, when First Lord of the Admiralty, closed the college down. Because George was a cadet he was excluded from a civil trial and had not reached the status for a court-martial so the Admiralty arranged an investigation. But George was not allowed to be represented and there was no opportunity for cross-examining witnesses who gave evidence against him. Accordingly,

---

6. Just over 75 pence.

Carson resorted to an archaic legal device called a Petition of Right against the Crown to bring the matter before the High Court.

A writ of claim was issued which came before Mr Justice Ridley in the Court of King's Bench on 12 July 1910. Carson led for the plaintiff, George's father, and Sir Rufus Isaacs, the Solicitor-General, for the Crown. Isaacs took the preliminary point of law that a Petition of Right was not appropriate. He relied upon the immunity of the Crown from legal proceedings and its absolute right to dismiss anyone who had entered its service. In spite of Carson's objections the judge entered judgment for the Crown on the point of law and that meant the case would not be heard. Carson was incensed and said, "This is a case of the grossest oppression without remedy that I have known since I have been at the Bar". He picked up his papers and stalked out of court. He then lodged an appeal and the case was sent back for rehearing, this time before Mr Justice Phillimore and a special jury.

"A Thief and a Forger"

A little boy of 13, Carson, told the jury, had been branded as a thief and a forger, "labelled and ticketed" as such for the rest of his life. In regard to the report of the handwriting expert called by the Crown Carson immediately clashed with the judge.

"Perhaps, gentlemen", he remarked to the jury, "I will have an opportunity of asking Mr Gurrin questions as to evidence given by him on other occasions".

"That observation is unworthy of you, Sir Edward", said the judge who was beginning to lean heavily on the side of the Crown. "Everybody knows Mr Gurrin".

"I resent that observation, my Lord", replied Carson. "I hope you will at once withdraw it".

The judge looked surprised. "I cannot do that, Sir Edward", he said

Looking away from the judge, Carson then said to the jury, "Well then, I do not mind it, gentlemen; I shall try not to become upset in this case, and will try to do my duty".

When George gave evidence he reiterated his innocence and during two days of gruelling cross-examination by Isaacs his evidence remained unshaken. The postmistress, on the other hand, was shown by Carson to be someone who could easily have been mistaken. She admitted that to her all the cadets looked alike and that, whilst dealing with one cadet and her other duties, another could have taken his place without her noticing. Furthermore, she was unable to point out George from among other cadets.

The Judge Advocate of the Fleet was called and Carson objected to the admissibility of his evidence since his inquiry had not been held in the presence of the boy.

"All this was done behind our backs", he said.

"Once for all", said the judge. "I say that I do not take the view that this was done any more behind your back than behind the back of the Crown".

"That is nothing to me", replied Carson. "The Crown was not being tried".

Carson then pointedly asked Mr Acland, who sat as a recorder,

"When you try a prisoner as recorder you hear both sides, I suppose".

"Yes", came the reply.

In view of all that was revealed it was not long before Isaacs told the court that the Admiralty now accepted that George Archer-Shee was innocent. The reason for the Admiralty's capitulation, namely that they were not going to succeed, became clear when members of the jury clambered out of the jury box to congratulate the plaintiff and his counsel.

The case had become a *cause célèbre* which swept the country but the Admiralty never expressed any regret and only reluctantly paid compensation of £3,000 and costs of £4,120 to the family after the matter was raised in the House of Commons and a tribunal set up. When war came George was unable to join the navy but enlisted in the army. He was killed, aged 19, in the battle of Ypres on the Western Front in 1914. His, and Carson's, fight for justice was dramatised by Terence Rattigan in a successful play, later a film, *The Winslow Boy*.

Ulster's "Strong Man"

Lloyd George's Parliament Act of 1911 ensured that Ireland's place in the United Kingdom could no longer be protected by the opposition of the House of Lords to Home Rule[7] since it provided that henceforth the lords could only delay and not reject legislation upon which the government of

---

7. Whereby Ireland would enjoy self-government but as a devolved part of the United Kingdom.

the day had set its mind. Carson, therefore, now turned to Ulster where, at an open-air rally on 23 September 1911, an estimated 100,000 people gathered to hear Carson and acclaim him as their new leader. In the event of a Home Rule Bill being passed, he told them, they must be prepared to become responsible for the government of the Protestant Province of Ulster.[8] The speech caused a sensation in Britain as well as Ireland and gave rise to the birth and arming of the Ulster Volunteer Force.

A year later Carson introduced the "Solemn League and Covenant" to spearhead resistance to Home Rule for Ireland. On 28 September 1912 all Belfast's factories and shipyards were closed and the day was turned over to the ceremony of signing the Covenant drawn up by Carson. He led a march to City Hall with a faded yellow banner said to have been King Billy's at the Battle of the Boyne. Escorting him, in familiar Orange tradition, was a guard of honour made up of 2,500 men in bowler hats carrying walking sticks. Carson defiantly breathed treason and with a silver pen was the first to sign the Covenant, followed by over 470,000 men and women supporters. Civil war loomed, with illegal gun-running and the Curragh Mutiny. Nevertheless, with a Home Rule Bill before Parliament Carson proposed that if it were passed the nine counties of Ulster should be excluded. This suggestion and its consequences eventually led to the separation of six counties of Northern Ireland as a province of the United Kingdom. But first the outbreak of the First World War saved Ulster from its own bloodbath.

Nevertheless, when, after the war, Ireland was partitioned by the Government of Ireland Act of 1922, with six of the counties becoming Northern Ireland, Carson felt his life's work for Ireland had been betrayed. On 14 December that year he made a bitter impromptu statement in the House of Lords in which he claimed he had been a puppet in the political game. In particular he turned upon his former friend and ally F E Smith ("Galloper Smith"), then sitting only a few feet away on the Woolsack as Lord Birkenhead, describing him as a loathsome man who sold his friends when he had got into power.

---

8. John Hostettler. *Sir Edward Carson—A Dream Too Far. Op. cit.* p. 166.

"Father of Northern Ireland"

Despite his service in the War Cabinet during World War I, at its end Carson had resumed his practice at the Bar and at the end of May 1921 had taken his place in the House of Lords as Baron Carson of Duncairn in the County of Antrim, one of the lords of appeal. Before long, however, he was again missing the limelight and referred to the House of Lords as a place "into which the rays of the sun never penetrate".

By 1929 his health was visibly fading and at the age of 75 he retired from the House of Lords. He died on 22 October 1935 and was provided with a state funeral in a Belfast that was closed and silent for the ceremony. He was buried in St. Anne's Cathedral and when the coffin was lowered into the tomb soil from each of the six counties was scattered on it.

Although his dream of preserving the union of Ireland with Britain has gone Carson's name continues to arouse fierce passions on all sides in Ireland even today. Like Cicero and others we shall meet in this book, he is a prime example of the role of successful lawyers who enter the field of power and politics where although influential they are less sure of success. The idea of a leading silk, involved in high profile cases, being an active member of the Lloyd George War Cabinet in the First World War, after declining the Woolsack, is extraordinary. And, once fêted as the "Uncrowned King of Ulster" Carson is still today often described as the "Father of Northern Ireland".

Considering Carson's role in Northern Ireland which helped cause the partition of the country, it is ironic in that his lifelong passion was to keep the whole of Ireland united as an integral part of the United Kingdom and British Empire.

Chapter 3

William Howe and Abraham Hummel
Tricksters and Criminals

For reasons that will become plain, these two fabulous USA lawyers must be taken together. And what a contrast they make to Clarence Darrow in *Chapter 1*. One a great as well as famous man and these two, although famous and colourful, they can only be described as despicable. They were a kind of double act on a vaudeville stage, but with a deeply sinister aspect. In truth, William F Howe and Abraham Hummel were glorified tricksters. Yet, Judge James B Wallace writing of them said they were,

> Bon vivants, boulevardiers, barristers extraordinary, they were gems in a setting that long since has been cast into the crucible of time. They have no counterparts today. Conditions in our modern Eden do not favour the flowering of such genius.[1]

Certainly there is no questioning the fact that despite their flawed characters they were the most well-known criminal lawyers in New York in their day in the late 19th-century. They defended over 1,000 defendants on charges of murder and manslaughter with Howe appearing for more than 650 of them.

Tricksters and Criminals
In fact, Howe and Hummel had a near monopoly of all the criminal business of New York at the time. They were the attorneys for all the major brothel

---
1. Richard H Rovere (1948), *Howe & Hummel: Their True and Scandalous History,* London: Michael Joseph, p. 8.

owners. "When 74 madams were rounded up during a purity drive in 1884, every one of them named Howe & Hummel as counsel".[2]

The two lawyers had in addition the business of

> every free-lance safe cracker, forger, arsonist, confidence man, bucket shop proprietor, and panel thief whose business was worth having. Howe & Hummel were the mouthpieces—if not, as was often asserted, the brains—of organized crime in New York for more than 30 years.[3]

Undoubtedly, their success was built not only on sharp brains but also on a strong element of criminality.

Howe's Early Life

William Howe was probably born in London in 1828 but little is known about his early years although he appears to have taken a great interest in celebrated murder trials at the Old Bailey at that time. Moreover, there is in the "Proceedings of the Old Bailey" a trial recorded in 1854 which featured a William Howe, and Howe is known to have had a criminal record and been in prison in England before arriving in New York in 1858 as a ticket of leave man, i.e. on parole. It seems almost certain that the man on trial was our William Howe. At the Old Bailey, where he described himself as a clerk to Reuben Simpson, attorney-at-law, he was charged with conspiracy with others to secure the discharge of Mary Ann Blatchford who was in custody on a charge of felony. Howe was found guilty and sentenced to 18 months' imprisonment.[4] It has been suggested that he had committed murder in London before fleeing to America but there is no other mention of him in the Old Bailey Proceedings which cover some 197,745 criminal trials and are unlikely to have omitted a murder trial. At all events he appears to have retained a cockney accent throughout his life.

---

2. *Ibid.* p. 19.
3. *Ibid.* pp. 19-20.
4. Old Bailey Proceedings Online: www.oldbaileyonline.org 18 September 1854. Ref: t18540918-997 (Accessed 26 June 2011).

Contrasting Pair

In 1869, Abraham Hummel joined Howe in partnership in New York and the two of them, "Howe the Lawyer" and "Little Abe" as they were described, made a striking pair. Howe was a man of enormous frame and girth and lion-headed with a walrus moustache. At six feet tall he was noted for his extravagant dress and the large number of diamonds and rings he wore even in court, unless the nature of the case demanded otherwise which was infrequently. In one trial he wore "so many diamonds on his scarf and turquoises and rubies scattered about that he fairly sparkled".[5] He was well-known for his oratory which was often over the top but successful in the New York courts of the day.

Hummel, on the other hand, was a genius, rake-thin, owlish and only five feet tall. He had a huge pear-shaped bald head and was fussy and crafty. He was a bachelor and looked like a hunchback but he too was always well turned out and did not scorn the use of diamonds although not wearing them on the same scale as Howe.

On the whole Howe dealt with the criminal side of the firm's work and appeared in court in some 650 or more murder trials and he was never squeamish about defending the most atrocious and bloody murderers. Hummel handled the civil cases of the firm and was brilliant at spotting loopholes in the law. In these criminal activities they were a perfect pair and one newspaper described Howe sweeping into view whilst,

> Lawyer Hummel trotted briskly along at his side, a black sprite with little black legs. In the corridors, [Howe's] diamond studded matchbox was much in evidence, and a death's-head with diamond eyes grinned from his watch chain.[6]

It is not known if either Howe or Hummel trained as lawyers. It seems unlikely that they did so and that would not have been unusual at the time. It was said that the criminal bar in New York consisted mainly of unfrocked

---

5. Cait Murphy. (2010), *Scoundrels in Law: The Trials of Howe & Hummel, Lawyers to the Gangsters, Cops, Starlets, and Rakes Who Made the Gilded Age*, New York: Harper Collins Publishers, p. 90.
6. Richard H Rovere, *Howe & Hummel: Their True and Scandalous History. Op. cit.* p. 29.

priests, drunkards, ex-police magistrates and all types of riff-raff.[7] The courts were full of lawyers with no academic training and a short time in the office of a member of the Bar would have been sufficient to enable an enterprising criminal to start up his own practice. It was enough to enable the abilities in the law of Howe and Hummel to become the stuff of legend.

Manipulators of the Law

Quite clearly they both understood the law and they knew how to manipulate it. People were taken up from the street to sign affidavits to destroy the credibility of opposing witnesses who were appearing in court. One criminal, Owen Reilly, was a serial arsonist. Following his arrest and being charged with arson he instructed Howe as his defending counsel. After reading the statues on arson Howe had his client plead guilty to attempted arson and both the district attorney and the judge accepted this lesser plea. To their surprise Howe then declared that as the sentence for attempted arson was half the maximum imposed for actual arson there could be no penalty. The punishment for arson was life imprisonment and how, asked Howe, could the court determine half-a-life? Would it be half a minute or half the life of Methuselah? The court accepted its defeat, Reilly walked away a free man and the arson statutes were changed.

Howe was also famous for bringing into court the mothers, wives and children of defendants on trial. And if the family of the accused were uncomely, Howe had a stable of homely-looking wives and children ready to call upon at short notice. On one occasion, in his first murder trial, when the prosecution brought into court the widows of three murdered men, Howe, used his wife and daughter who were in court in his defence of the accused who was charged with murder by poisoning. Indeed, the prisoner admitted killing the three men and offered to plead guilty to manslaughter but the prosecution, foolishly as it turned out, insisted on proceeding with the charge of murder. Warming to his task and pointing to his own wife and daughter with tears streaming down his face, Howe asked the jury, "Will you on the sole authority of this disreputable scullion make that woman a widow — that child an orphan"? With this shameless hoax on Howe's part the accused was found

---

7. Arthur Train. (1908) *True Stories of Crime From the District Attorney's Office.* London, T. Werner Laurie.

not guilty.[8] Frequently, children who had no connection with the defendant were shown how to cuddle up to the prisoner and smother him or her with kisses and tears.

One New York newspaper wrote that one of Howe's most audacious defences occurred with,

> his sudden turn in the trial of Edward Unger, who confessed that he had killed a lodger, cut up the body, thrown part in the East River, and sent the rest in a box to Baltimore. Mr Howe stupefied the courtroom by dramatically denying that Unger had done any of those things. He increased the surprise by asserting that Unger's little seven-year-old girl, at that moment on her father's knee, had done them. After tapping thus a wellspring of astonishment, Mr Howe turned the emotion dextrously into profound sympathy by explaining that it was the thought of the little girl which prompted Unger to conceal a deed done in the heat of passion. The jury convicted the confessed murderer of manslaughter only.[9]

In fact, Howe told the jury, Unger had not really dismembered the body at all. The hand had been his, but the force that guided the hand was his daughter whom Unger was dangling on his knee in the courtroom.

One young lawyer, however, succeeded in beating Howe in a jury trial. Addressing the jury at the close of a trial, he said,

> Gentlemen, I am shocked to see that you were not indignant over the sickening flattery that has come from the lips of Mr Howe. Now I do not, as he pretends to do, consider you the brainiest and handsomest men in the world, but merely as belonging to the ordinary run of mortals. But I can see from your self-satisfied faces that there will be a miscarriage of justice by the acquittal of this prisoner ... But I must tell you this sequel: after the scandalous acquittal which will follow your deliberations in the jury room, I shall have a visitation from this man Howe. He will be once again arrayed in the diamonds he wore here on the first day of the trial, and there will be a wide grin substituted for the tears you have seen. There will be nothing lachrymose about him as he plants himself in a comfortable chair

---

8. *Ibid.* pp. 57-8.
9. *New York Tribune,* 2 September 1902.

in my office and, with his feet up on my desk, delivers himself of this estimate of you: 'Horace, what perfect dammed fools these jurors are'.[10]

After that Howe lost the case but no other barrister ever challenged him before a jury in the same manner.

Famous Clients

While Howe was undermining the character of witnesses, making outrageous statements in court and juggling with jurors in trials of bank robbers and murderers Hummel was helping gamblers and fraudsters to outwit the law. The civil side to the firm's practice, dealt with mainly by Hummel, was also extensive and well-paid. On one occasion Hummel discovered a technical error in the committal proceedings against 240 petty criminals. He collected a fee from each of them and secured the release of them all from the prison at Blackwell's Island. To assist the process the two lawyers bribed the judge but when this was revealed no action was taken to disbar them. Perhaps they bribed another judge. They were certainly believed to be directing criminal operations on a grand scale.

The firm were also the leading divorce and theatrical lawyers. Among their theatrical clients were to be found P T Barnum, John Barrymore, Henry Irving, John Drew and Lily Langtry as well as other well-known celebrities. At the same time Hummel was himself a persistent blackmailer. Indeed, the firm was widely known for engaging in blackmail, incitement to perjury, the fabricating of evidence and the bribery of judges, jurors and public officials. These crimes were clearly revealed in court yet until Hummel's end no action was ever taken against them—probably from fear of the consequences at their hands.

Moreover, Hummel could be clever and subtle. In a case of alleged indecency involving what the prosecution described as an obscene dance he claimed it originated in ancient Greece and portrayed religious bliss. It was, he said, "[A] favourite of the Khedive of Egypt … it symbolized the religion and poetry of the mysterious East, a classical dance of profound religious significance that imitated the movements of the planets and had been sanctified

---

10. Richard H. Rovere, *Howe and Hummel: Their True and Scandalous History, Op. cit*, p. 68.

by history". However, in an unusual failure by Hummel the dancers were found guilty, fined $50 dollars each and told to go and sin no more.[11]

Hummel Brought Down

Eventually, on 2 September 1902 Howe, a heavy drinker, and after several heart attacks, died in his sleep at home on Boston Road in the Bronx. Hummel continued the firm with two of his former assistants but his end as a lawyer came with the complicated Dodge-Morse case.

In the usual Howe and Hummel style, Hummel had persuaded witnesses to commit perjury and had indulged in other malpractices, admitting at one point that he was a crook and a blackmailer. Pursued over ten months in a spectacular manhunt by William Jerome, a first cousin of Winston Churchill and the district attorney of New York County, Hummel was finally brought to trial in January 1905 and, after attempting to bribe some of the jurors, he was found guilty and sentenced to pay a fine of 100 dollars and spend a year in prison on Blackwell's Island. His disbarment followed and the firm ceased to practice.

After his release from prison Hummel travelled to London with an estimated one million dollars and a fine send off by prominent Americans. Crime appears to have paid and in London he lived in luxury in Grosvenor Square. He also travelled frequently to Paris and may have bought a chain of cinemas there. He died in Baker Street on 21 January 1926 and his body was taken back to the USA where it was buried in Salem Fields Cemetery in the Queens' district of New York. But his memory lives on. Both he and Howe are still part of the folklore of the New York Bar.

---

11. Cait Murphy, *Scoundrels in Law: The Trials of Howe & Hummel, Lawyers to the Gangsters, Cops, Starlets, and Rakes Who Made the Gilded Age*, Op. cit, pp. 201-2.

Chapter 4

Matthew Hale
Judge, Jurist, Writer, Reformer

Momentous Times
Sir Matthew Hale lived through the momentous 17th-century struggles between the Crown and Parliament that produced the English civil war, the execution of Charles I, the rule of Oliver Cromwell and the restoration of the monarchy. It was a time of dramatic events that changed the political face of Britain and sowed the seeds for the future rise of democracy in its modern form. At this vitally important time Hale played a significant role as an advocate, a Member of Parliament, a jurist and a judge. He was the pre-eminent lawyer of the day and his life bears witness to a pivotal interaction of history, politics and law. His place in history survives because of his understanding and exposition of the crucial bedrock function of the Rule of Law in the flexible and changing Constitution of this country.

Early Years
Hale was born in the village of Alderley in Gloucestershire on 1 November 1609. When five-years-of-age he was orphaned by the loss of both his father and his mother. He was then brought up by a strict Puritan guardian and, for his education, placed with a Puritan schoolmaster known as "The Scandalous Vicar" on account of his religious extremism. The indoctrination to which the young and impressionable Matthew was subjected led to the only serious blot on his career as a judge when he was involved in the infamous witchcraft trial in Bury St Edmunds in 1665. In the meantime, however, at

the age of 17 he began his studies of the law at Magdalen Hall, Oxford and on 8 November 1629 he was admitted to Lincoln's Inn.

Advocate

Hale was soon seen as a brilliant and extremely successful advocate. He was much in demand and in 1641, as the best constitutional lawyer in the kingdom, he defended Charles I's friend, the Earl of Strafford, on his attainder by Parliament for high treason in attempting to bring over from Ireland an army to buttress the monarchy. With Hale's help, Strafford pleaded eloquently and with great skill and courage but the outcome could not be in doubt when he was abandoned by the king. He was executed in May 1641.

Subsequently, Hale was retained as counsel (with John Herne) for the ultra-royalist Archbishop William Laud, on his impeachment by the House of Commons in October 1644.[1] The archbishop was charged at Common Law with high treason in subverting the fundamental laws of England, the Protestant religion and the privileges of Parliament. Hale argued that nothing Laud was alleged to have said or done amounted to treason and that the Statute of Treason of 1352 had abolished all Common Law treasons. Indeed, it was a political trial and Serjeant Wilde, for the prosecution, admitted that no single crime of Laud's amounted to treason or even felony but contended that all his misdemeanours together made many treasons. Herne retorted, "I crave your mercy, good Mr Serjeant. I never understood before this time that 200 couple of black rabbits would make a black horse!" According to Lord Chancellor Finch, Herne made the arguments for Laud but they were written by Hale.[2]

One historian, Clayton Roberts, has written that in the whole of the 17th-century no counsel made a more destructive attack on the validity of Common Law and constructive and declaratory treasons outside the Statute of Treason than did the lawyers assisting Laud, "the most influential of whom, was the young Matthew Hale." Five of the nine lords who attended the House in January 1645 interpreted the law differently from Laud's lawyers and condemned him to death because, "The House of Commons demanded it, the London mob clamoured for it and the Lords had not the conviction

---

1. Howell, *State Trials*.(1812), vol. iv. p. 315.
2. *Ibid*. pp. 577 and 586.

to stand against it."³ With his own forthcoming trial in mind Laud had earlier lamented that Strafford had died with more honour than any of those who hunted after his life would gain.⁴

Rule by Red Gowns

When Charles I was charged with treason Hale was prepared to defend him and is believed to have advised him when he refused to accept the jurisdiction of the court. That meant, however, that no defence was possible. Charles was found guilty and executed outside the Banqueting Hall in Whitehall. Ten days later Hale was defending James, Duke of Hamilton and Earl of Cambridge, on his trial for high treason before the Upper Court presided over by John Bradshaw who had been president of the commission which tried the king. "Upper Court" was the new name for the Court of King's Bench, and was widely known as, "Cromwell's New Slaughter-house in England".⁵

The truncated House of Commons also abolished the House of Lords, as being "useless and dangerous"⁶ as well as the oaths of allegiance and supremacy and it had declared England to be a Republic and free Commonwealth. Coins were issued with the words, "The Commonwealth of England" on one side and "God with us" on the other. This led to the jest that God and the Commonwealth were not on the same side.

Only six of the Common Law judges accepted commissions under Cromwell. Hale did so reluctantly and only after Cromwell had told him that he desired to rule by the laws of the land, but added, "If you will not let me govern by red gowns I am resolved to govern by red coats".⁷

Trial of the Duke of Hamilton

The Duke of Hamilton was accused of leading a Scottish army into England in support of the king in 1648. It was this army that was defeated at

---

3. Clayton Roberts (1966), *The Growth of Responsible Government in Stuart England*, p. 131.
4. C V Wedgwood (1964), *Thomas Wentworth: First Earl of Strafford 1593-1641, A Revaluation*. London: Jonathan Cape, p. 380.
5. William Cobbett (1809), *State Trials*, vol. iii, p. 1155.
6. Cromwell and a third of the MPs had wished to retain the Lords as a consultative body. S R Gardiner (1894), *History of the Commonwealth and Protectorate, 1649-1660*, vol. I, p. 3.
7. Sollom Emlyn (1736), Preface to Hale's *History of the Pleas of the Crown*, London: E and R Nutt and R Gosling, vol. i. p. 2.

Preston by Cromwell and the New Model Army and it was then that the Duke was taken prisoner. He was subsequently held in Windsor but escaped from captivity and managed to reach London. There he was arrested by a party of soldiers. On being questioned by them, he attempted to light his pipe with some incriminating papers which they seized. On his appearance in court charged with treason by levying war against the Commonwealth he had no counsel and Hale and three other lawyers were assigned by the judge to defend him.

Hale spoke "elaborately and at length" in his defence.[8] The essence of his defence was that since Hamilton was a Scot he owed allegiance only to Scotland which was a separate country with its own system of law. It was the Scottish Parliament which had sent him across the border, and thus he could not be guilty of treason in England. According to the *State Trials* the prosecuting counsel pleaded, "so poorly that all who heard them were ashamed; but they had one advantage, that neither the Duke nor his counsel were allowed to speak after them". Moreover, as the Earl of Cambridge, Hamilton was an English peer and since he was born after the accession to the throne of James I he was considered in law to be a natural-born Englishman. In *Calvin's Case* in 1609 the judges had decided that persons born in Scotland after the accession of James IV to the English throne as James I were to be so regarded.[9] Accordingly Hamilton was found guilty and beheaded on a scaffold before the gate of Westminster Hall.

Love's Plot

Christopher Love, a popular Presbyterian minister who had been chaplain at Windsor Castle, was charged with high treason in plotting with others against the Commonwealth, raising forces against the government and corresponding with the future Charles II. It is significant that he was accused of sending letters to Charles II before a statute made it unlawful to do so. He was brought to trial on various dates in May, June and July 1651[10] before the High Court of Justice which had been set up in the previous year to try cases of treason against the Commonwealth without the "burden" of a

---

8. William Cobbett. *State Trials. Op. cit.* col. 1162.
9. 7 Co. Rep. At f3b.
10. William Cobbett. (1810) *State Trials.* vol. v. cols. 43-268.

jury. Described as a "new Star Chamber with powers of life and death",[11] of its first 64 members only three were lawyers, although Parliament quickly added six judges.

Although Love pleaded not guilty he was denied counsel and prosecution witnesses were produced who gave evidence implicating him, although they appeared to do so reluctantly. Love argued that they had been threatened with death if they did not give evidence against him. One witness who was called to testify against him, a minister named Jackson, declined to do so and was fined £500 and imprisoned in The Fleet gaol. At length after Love had raised questions of law the court agreed that he should engage counsel and, at his request, Hale was assigned by the court as one of them, once again as the principal advocate.

Initially Hale asked for an adjournment as he had seen his client for the first time that morning and had not been allowed to see the full charge. Asked by Mr Justice Keble if he had ever heard of a prisoner being given a copy of the charge Hale replied that he knew from personal knowledge that the charges against them had been supplied to both Strafford and Laud whom he had represented. Notwithstanding, no copy of the charge was made available.

The indictment, urged Hale, was incomplete as it did not contain allegations that Love had committed acts of treason—which had been raised only in prosecution evidence. This was a plea of considerable importance at that time when if an indictment was at all flawed the trial could not proceed. In a less highly-charged trial this is what would have happened but the court proceeded regardless. Hale also argued that the charge was invalidated by the inclusion of acts alleged to have been committed before the relevant statute was enacted. He further pointed out that the prosecution had not produced two competent witnesses against Love as was required by the law of treason.

Despite the validity of these points of law, Love was found guilty and sentenced to be beheaded. At this petitions flowed into Parliament asking that he be pardoned and he was granted a reprieve for a little over a month. A petition for mercy was then sent to Cromwell who was at war in Scotland and it was widely accepted that he replied by letter consenting to a pardon. Unfortunately for Love, the messenger bearing the letter was seized by a

---

11. S R Gardiner, *History of the Commonwealth and Protectorate, 1649-1660. Op. cit,* vol. I, p. 277.

group of Cavalier soldiers who destroyed it. In the absence of the letter he was executed on Tower Hill on 22 August. Shortly before his death Love praised the ability of Hale which he attributed to "divine assistance".[12] Three months later nine of his alleged accomplices who acknowledged their guilt were pardoned.

The Hale Commission

During Cromwell's Commonwealth, Hale was appointed, on 30 January 1652, to act as chairman of what became known as the Hale Commission. Although he took the chair on only ten occasions and attended 25 out of 59 meetings his influence on the Commission was considerable. It was charged by the House of Commons to propose reforms in the law and present its opinions to a committee of the House.[13] The Commission, made up of lawyers, gentry, merchants and army officers, included Major-General Desborough, an attorney, and Cromwell's brother-in-law; Hugh Peters, a dedicated law reformer and scourge of the lawyers; the influential John Rushworth and Sir Anthony Ashley Cooper (afterwards Lord Shaftesbury). They produced 16 Bills which were presented to the Parliamentary Law Committee in July 1652. Both the Law Committee and the House of Commons proved to be sympathetic but they did not manage to secure the enactment of a single one. Nonetheless, many of the Commission's proposals were adopted during the succeeding century-and-a-half.

For example, a sweeping reduction in the use of capital punishment was introduced by Lord John Russell in 1837, prisoners were finally permitted to engage counsel to appear for them in 1836 and their witnesses were allowed to give evidence on oath in 1702. The torture of pressing to death (*peine forte et dure*) was abolished in 1827 as was the burning of women felons at the stake in 1790 and benefit of clergy in 1827. A Court of Appeal had been called for as was a small-claims court. All these, and other reforms, had been argued for by the Commission and were eventually achieved by later generations.

---

12. Christopher Love (1651), *A Clear and Necessary Vindication of Mr Love's Principles and Practices*, p. 42.
13. House of Commons Journals, vol. vii, p. 58.

Witchcraft

Hale played no part in the trial of Charles I and after the Restoration he endeavoured to persuade the House of Commons to ensure that Charles II kept his promise of religious toleration. But his efforts were defeated by General Monke who had secured the return of the king. However, despite having served under Cromwell, and his attempt to limit the royal prerogative, Hale was widely revered as a judge and he was appointed Lord Chief Baron of the Exchequer on 7 November 1660.

It was in this role that there occurred the only noticeable blot on Hale's career. On 10 March 1665 two elderly widows, Rose Callender and Amy Duny, were brought to trial before the Lord Chief Baron and a jury at the Bury St Edmunds Assizes in Suffolk.[14] They were charged with the statutory crime of witchcraft. Seven children who were said to be too young or allegedly too ill to give evidence were brought into court. Immediately they fell into fits and were struck dumb. As a consequence, their parents gave bizarre evidence about events six or seven years earlier that included the children spitting up 40 or more pins on single occasions. Among other things they were said to have seen invisible mice and ducks and one child was said to have had a nail put in her mouth by a bee that in reality was a witch.

Several eminent men who were in court, including Serjeant John Kelyng who later became chief justice of the King's Bench, examined the children, with Hale's permission, and declared that they were imposters. Indeed, Kelyng declared he was "much dissatisfied" with the evidence which was not sufficient to convict the prisoners who, he declared, should not be found guilty upon "the imagination only of the parties bewitched. For if that might be allowed, no person whatsoever can be in safety, for perhaps they might fancy another person, who might altogether be innocent in such matters".[15] At the conclusion of the evidence, Hale addressed the jury but declined to repeat the evidence.

Ignoring the conclusions of the eminent men, including Kelyng, Hale then added that there undoubtedly were witches because the scriptures affirmed it and there were laws that made it a crime. Indeed, chapter 22(18) of the *Book of Exodus* reads, "Thou shall not suffer a witch to live" and chapter 22(27)

---

14. William Cobbett, *State Trials, Op. cit*, vol. vi, col. 647.
15. *Ibid*. col. 690.

of *Leviticus,* "A man also or a woman that hath a familiar spirit, or that is a wizard, shall surely be put to death; they shall stone them with stones; their blood *shall* be upon them". Being a man of his time and deeply religious Hale took these texts to heart but he should not have taken seriously the tissue of lies, children's fantasies and pitiful "proofs" of witchcraft in the case, particularly as not all his brother judges at the time were equally disposed to heed such nonsense and dispense justice from the *Bible* instead of the law.

It took the jury only half an hour to find both women guilty and within another half-an-hour all the children were perfectly able to speak and were in good health. Hale sentenced the women to be hanged and the poor wretches were executed on 17 March 1664 still protesting their innocence. Subsequent judges and jurists have described the trial as an enormous violation of justice as indeed it was. It was also a wretched episode that marred Hale's integrity and otherwise distinguished career.

Law Reform
At this time Hale returned to the question of law reform with his *Of the Alteration, Amendment or Reformation of the Lawes of England.*[16] In this he argued that since everything on earth was subject to change, abuses and corruptions grew into the law over time and had to be removed. He wrote that in the interests of society, as customs, contracts, commerce and the tempers of men and societies changed in the long term, so should the laws be changed to keep them useful. Not that this justified wholesale change. The Common Law was settled and understood and an entirely new system would be either too rigid or too fluid; too narrow or too wide and interpreting it would disrupt the existing framework. Nevertheless, the law could be codified by Parliament and have fewer flaws than was common.

On a practical level Hale made a number of suggestions for reform. Suits for debt or damages of less than £10 should be withdrawn from the higher courts at Westminster and held in the county and hundred courts in the localities. Overall what was needed was:

1. County courts in all places.

---
16. Hargrave (1665), *Tracts,* BL, *Add MSS,* 18,234.

2. In each county a barrister of at least seven years' standing should be appointed as steward for the county with a fixed fee.
3. The steward to sit as a judge of the court with a jury of 12 men.
4. There should be six attorneys permitted for each county who would be appointed (or removed) by the Chief Justice of the Common Pleas.
5. The courts should deal with causes involving up to £5 excluding those where title to freehold or leasehold land was in question.

Sir William Holdsworth, who regarded Hale as the first of our great modern lawyers, said of this work that "It is safe to say that no wiser tract on this topic has ever been written in the whole course of the history of English law".[17]

The History of the Pleas of the Crown

During the course of his lifetime Hale wrote many millions of words having spent 40 years collecting the magnificent library of manuscripts and books from which he produced most of his numerous written works. His major and most important work, *The History of the Pleas of the Crown*, was published in 1736, a century after the death of Sir Edward Coke, and also after his own death.

From early times pleas of the Crown were grave capital offences alleged in indictments to have been committed "against the peace of our Lord the King, his Crown and dignity". They were triable only in the king's courts and not in the county and hundred courts. In this work of 1,124 pages Hale to some extent followed Coke's *Third Institute* in his divisions of the criminal law, his statement of the principles of the law and with many of the cases cited. On the other hand, the *Pleas of the Crown* was far more methodical, comprehensive, penetrating and modern than the *Institute*.

Comparing the *Pleas of the Crown* with the *Institute* the Victorian jurist and judge, Sir James Fitzjames Stephen, considered that Hale's treatise was "not only of the highest authority but shows a depth of thought and a comprehensiveness of design which puts it in quite a different category from Coke's *Institute*". He added that, "it is written on an excellent plan, and is far more

---
17. Sir William Holdsworth (1966), *A History of English Law*, vol. vi. p. 592.

of a treatise and far less of an index or mere work of practice than any book on the subject known to me".[18] Nevertheless, Hale had Coke's *Institute* to build on and it is clear from his *Pleas of the Crown* that he owed a real debt to Coke whom Stephen appears to have underestimated.

Even as recently as 1993, giving judgment in the case of *R. v. Kingston*[19] judges of the Court of Appeal said that they relied upon Hale's "classic statement of principle" on drunkenness as a defence to a criminal charge. Earlier Lord Denning had similarly cited from the *Pleas of the Crown* in the case of *Attorney-General for Northern Ireland v. Gallagher*.[20] Thus does the memory and work of this outstanding advocate, jurist, judge and law reformer remain undimmed with his treatise still regarded as of high authority.

---

18. James Fitzjames Stephen (1883). *A History of the Criminal Law of England*. vol. ii, p. 211.
19. (1993) 157 *Justice of the Peace Reports*. p. 1171.
20. (1961) 3 All ER.

Chapter 5

Marcus Tullius Cicero
Birth of the Rule of Law

Servant of the Law

Marcus Cicero was born in 106 BC in Arpinum (now Arpino) some 70 miles south of Rome. Rome was a sophisticated city with over a million inhabitants and it was here that he received his education in philosophy, rhetoric and law. It was law, however, which, along with politics, were to provide the essential elements in his career. At this period of the Republic, Rome was in the hands of cliques of great and rich families under whom it was speedily moving towards decay. Men like Cicero were excluded from these circles by both birth and limited resources. He was not from one of the great aristocratic families, he had no great wealth and, unlike Caesar, no great army to support him. But, using the law and his unparalleled eloquence, he attacked the violence and greed of the ruling groups at every opportunity and his success was unique in Roman history. He not only became a famous lawyer he was also a great one.

Speaking of the law he wrote,

> True law is Reason, right and natural, commanding people to fulfil their obligations and prohibiting and deterring them from doing wrong. Its validity is universal; it is immutable and eternal ... Neither the Senate nor the Assembly can exempt us from its demands.[1]

---
1. Marcus Tullius Cicero (1999), *On the Commonwealth and On the Laws* (ed. James E G Zetzel), Cambridge: Cambridge University Press.

He also wrote that, "We are servants of the law in order that we may be free".[2] It was in the service of the law and the Republic that he used his eloquence, "which is the foundation of all subsequent European prose".[3] And, although he was occasionally tempted to compromise as politicians do, he always had the Republic at heart and at one time was called the "Father of the Nation". To become a successful orator in Rome took many years but the rewards were great. At the time the force of argument and the power of persuasion could influence politicians and in the courts determine who would or would not be removed from public life. And of all the orators in the ancient world Cicero was probably the best.[4]

Early Rule of Law

In 79 BC Cicero travelled to Athens and Rhodes, in the equivalent of the later European "Grand Tour", before returning to Rome and his career in law and politics. He was elected as a *Quaestor* (magistrate) in 70 BC and served successfully in Sicily and as a junior senator in Rome before he was elected a *Praetor* (a more senior magistrate and judge) and in 63 BC he became one of two *Consuls,* the highest post in the Senate which was the supreme council of the Roman state. This was unusual for a "new man" who was not a member of the aristocracy in that hierarchical society.

Despite its defects, and in particular some bribery of juries, an early form of the Rule of Law operated in the Republic. Advocates appeared at trials held in the Forum and the jury courts, which decided upon alleged crimes of murder, treason, extortion and the like. And they also worked as private detectives collecting evidence and securing witnesses. In court there could be between 30 and 60 jurors presided over by a *Praetor* and "verdicts were often biased and bribery of jurors was common".[5] It was in such a court that Cicero began his legal career.

---

2. Marcus Tullius Cicero (1896), *Pro Cuentio* (ed. J D Maillard), London: W B Clive.
3. Michael Grant (1965), *Introduction to Cicero Selected Works,* London: Penguin Books, p. 20.
4. D H Berry (2008), *Cicero: Defence Speeches,* Oxford: Oxford University Press, p. xi.
5. Anthony Everitt (2003). *Cicero: The Life and Times of Rome's Greatest Politician,* New York: Random House Trade Paperbacks, p. 32.

Trial of Sextus Roscius

In 80 BC Sextus Roscius was charged with murdering his father.[6] Acting in his defence Cicero, aged 26, made his first speech in a criminal court. To do so was an act of bravery in the Rome of the dictator Sulla since the case could expose the corruption of Sulla's friends. Roscius's father, also named Sextus Roscius, was walking back from a dinner party one night when he was set upon and killed. He was a well-to-do farmer from Ameria some 50 miles north of Rome who left a considerable inheritance to his son on his death. However, his enemies plotted to secure the estate by accusing the son of murdering his father and disinheriting him. Lawyers approached by the son to act in his defence declined for fear of repercussions from Sulla.

Parricide was regarded by Romans as a particularly outrageous crime and if he were found guilty the horrendous punishment to be inflicted upon Roscius would involve being stripped, scourged, sewn up in a sack together with a dog, a cock, a viper and a monkey and being thrown into a river or the sea to be drowned.[7] In despair he asked the virtually unknown Cicero to take up the case.

The prosecution alleged that the son had killed his father to avoid being disinherited by him. However, in a lengthy speech Cicero turned the tables on the prosecutors and accused them of the murder. He also attacked Sulla's favourite, Chrysogonus, as the person behind the murder. In his peroration to the jury he said:

> Men who are wise, and endowed with the authority and power which you possess, have a particular duty to cure those ills from which our country is particularly suffering. There is no one among you who is not conscious that the Roman people, who used to be thought merciful to their enemies abroad, are currently suffering from cruelty at home. Remove this cruelty from our nation, gentlemen. Do not allow it to continue any longer in this country of ours. It is an evil thing, not only because it has done away with so many citizens in a most dreadful manner, but because it has taken away the feeling of compassion from even the mildest of men, by accustoming them to troubles. For when we are witnessing or hearing of some

---

6. D H Berry, *Cicero: Defence Speeches, Op. cit.* p. 3.
7. *Ibid.* p. 5.

dreadful event every hour, even those of us who are tender-hearted by nature find that, through constant contact with unpleasantness, we lose all sense of humanity.[8]

However, the mesmerising effect of Cicero's oratory on juries can only be appreciated by reading his long speech in full.

By accusing the accusers he obtained a brilliant victory when the jury acquitted Roscius and Cicero immediately became a foremost lawyer and orator of Rome, much sought after by litigants.

Prosecution of Caius Verres

Cicero usually acted for the defence but in another early trial he prosecuted so powerfully that his name reverberated throughout Rome. This was the trial in 70 BC of Caius Verres whose name had become a byword for corruption and theft during his three-year term as governor of Sicily in which he painstakingly and efficiently plundered that island. Verres used his position to steal large numbers of valuable sculptures and works of art from Sicilian local authorities and residents. In addition he also demanded much of their wealth. In particular, after having fleeced a distinguished citizen named Sthenius, he falsely accused him of forgery and fined him 500,000 sesterces — silver coins each worth perhaps the equivalent of one pound sterling. Sthenius fled to Rome where Verres followed him and laid a capital charge against him. A delegation from Sicily, where Cicero was well-known and well-regarded, appealed to him to charge Verres with extortion and he agreed. Verres appointed as his advocate the leading lawyer in Rome at the time, Quintus Hortensius Hortalus.

Cicero won a stay of trial for 110 days and travelled to Sicily in order to collect both evidence and witnesses but was met with strong opposition from the new governor Lucius Caecilius Metellus, an aristocratic crony of Verres. However, by hard work Cicero obtained all the witnesses and evidence he required and returned to Rome well within the time limit. There he found, however, that Verres and his supporters were working to secure delays in the trial in order to ensure that it would not end until friends of Verres had

---

8. *Ibid.* pp. 57-8.

been elected as Consuls and could influence the result. Cicero thought hard how to thwart these plans.

It was traditional for trials in Rome to start with long speeches by the advocates sometimes lasting for several weeks. To save time Cicero decided to dispense with his opening address and proceed directly to the evidence. With the evidence he had accumulated in Sicily he was able to reveal, with stunning eloquence and wit, that Verres had procured from its citizens, many of whom he impoverished, some 40 million sesterces. Lawful inheritances had been cancelled and seized. "Allies of unassailable loyalty," said Cicero,

> were treated as enemies; Roman citizens were tortured and put to death like slaves. Criminals of the deepest dye would bribe their way to acquittal, while men of impeccable honesty were prosecuted in their absence, and convicted and banished unheard.

Then again, "ancient monuments given by wealthy monarchs to adorn the cities of Sicily, or presented or restored to them by victorious Roman generals, were ravaged and stripped bare, one and all, by this same governor". He bought judges and the properties of farmers were seized and their owners robbed of countless sums.

> When I turn to his adulteries and similar outrages, continued Cicero, considerations of decency deter me from giving details of these loathsome manifestations of his lusts. Besides, I do not want, by describing them, to worsen the calamities of the people who have not been permitted to save their children and their wives from Verres' sexual passions.[9]

After Cicero's lengthy and passionate onslaught, Verres' counsel withdrew from the case and Verres fled into exile. The jury found him guilty and he was fined. At this point Hortensius returned to speak in mitigation for his friend. As a reward Verres gave him an ivory figurine of a sphinx. In the course of his own address in reply to Hortensius, Cicero made some enigmatic remark and Hortensius interrupted: "I am afraid I am no good at solving 'riddles'."

---

9. Michael Grant (1965). *Cicero: Selected Works, Op. cit.* pp. 41-43.

"Oh, really", snapped Cicero, "In spite of having a sphinx at home?"[10] This prosecution, which was a great forensic success, was another auspicious beginning to Cicero's legal and political career and quickly resulted in him becoming Rome's leading advocate in place of Hortensius.

Conspiracy

Another signal success was his foiling in 63 BC of a conspiracy to assassinate him and foment chaos in the city. Its purpose was to destroy the Republic and take control of the state. The leader of this proposed coup was Lucius Sergius Catilina, with the possible support of Julius Caesar. Cicero secured a declaration of martial law and with four vehement speeches known as the *Catiline Orations* outlining the plotters debaucheries he drove Catilina from the city. Catilina's followers continued, however, with their efforts to destroy the Republic from within whilst Catilina attacked the city from outside with a foreign army. But Cicero produced letters which incriminated five conspirators, and forced them to confess their crimes to the Senate. Caesar, as ever anti-Republican and opportunistic, pleaded with the Senate for leniency for the conspirators but the Senate agreed upon the death penalty and they were strangled in Rome's prison. In consequence Cicero received the accolade of "Father of the Country" but this honour was tempered by his fear that he might be tried for having put Roman citizens to death without trial in court.

Trial of Lucius Murena

With the conspiracy in the background, in the year 67 BC Lucius Murena, who was a prominent politician and general elected to succeed Cicero as Consul, was charged with malpractice in handing out bribes during the campaign for the consulship in the previous year. Cicero defended him with a speech of some humour. He scoffed at Marcus Porcius Cato, one of the prosecutors who attacked Cicero on several grounds, for his extravagant commitment to the uncomplaining fortitude in suffering demanded by Stoicism. He also commented that:

---

10. Anthony Everitt. *Cicero: The Life and Times of Rome's Greatest Politician. Op. cit.* p.79.

Cato argues with me on rigid and Stoical principles. He says that it is not right for goodwill to be enticed by food. He says that men's judgments, in the important business of electing men to office, ought not to be corrupted by pleasures. So, if a candidate invites a man to supper, he commits an offence. "Do you," he asks, "seek to obtain supreme power, supreme authority, and the helm of the Republic, by encouraging men's sensual appetites, by soothing their minds by offering them luxuries? Are you seeking employment as a pimp from a band of lecherous young men, or the sovereignty of the world from the Roman people?"

What an extraordinary thing to say! For our customs, our way of living, our manners, and the constitution itself reject it. Consider the Spartans, the inventors of that lifestyle and of that sort of language, men who lie down at mealtime on hard oak benches, and the Cretans, none of whom ever lies down at all to eat. Neither of them has preserved their political constitutions or their power better than the Romans, who set aside times for pleasure as well as times for work. One of those nations was destroyed by a single invasion of our army, the other only maintains its discipline and its laws thanks to our imperial protection.

Cato sourly observed: "What a comical Consul we've got!".[11] Mureno, who may well have been guilty, was acquitted in the national interest, as suggested by Cicero, he being an experienced general whose services were needed at the time when Rome was under threat. In 46-44 BC Cicero more or less retired and wrote most of his chief works on rhetoric and philosophy.

Murder of Cicero
In 60 BC Cicero turned down an invitation to join Julius Caesar, Pompey and Crassus in what was known as the First Triumvirate since he correctly believed it would undermine the Republic. This exposed him to the threat he feared when, in 58 BC, Publius Clodius Pulcher introduced a law to exile anyone who executed a Roman citizen without trial. As a result, Cicero was retrospectively condemned to exile in Greece and his homes were burned and plundered. Nonetheless, a year later, in 57 BC, the people of Rome voted for his return and he did so when recalled by the Senate.

---

11. *Ibid.* pp. 105-6.

After the assassination of Caesar, Cicero made an enemy of Mark Antony whom he attacked in a series of philippics. When Antony, Octavian and Lepidus formed the Second Triumvirate, Antony insisted that Cicero and his family be proscribed as enemies of the people and killed. Despite the fact that later he would effectively destroy the Republic, Octavian (later called Augustus) opposed the demand for two days but eventually he fell into line. As a direct consequence, in 43 BC, Cicero, old and weary, fled to his villa at the coast where he was pursued and overtaken by Antony's soldiers as he was being carried in a litter. Bravely putting his head out and defying the soldiers to do their worst he was murdered by decapitation and had his hands cut off.

In a Rome of violence in the destruction of the Republic this greatest lawyer of the ancient world, and eloquent defender of Republican institutions and the Rule of Law against authoritarian rule, had his voice finally silenced in the only manner possible — death. Thus died an orator who wrote poetry, a politician steeped in history and a man who defended clemency, democracy and the rights of free men under the law. His legacy has shone like a beacon of inspiration to western civilization.

Chapter 6

Henry Brougham
Glitz of Cannes to the Calm of the Woolsack

Advocate

Lord Brougham is considered by some to have been a champion of the people and by others as a glittering failure. Certainly his name and his career awaken interest in lawyers and laymen alike. Born in Edinburgh in 1778, his father was of an old Westmorland family and his mother a niece of the historian William Robertson. He went to the city's university at the age of 13 fired with an Enlightenment enthusiasm to acquire knowledge of every kind. His chosen field of study was to read humanities and philosophy which included natural philosophy, mathematics, ancient languages, political economy, rhetoric, logic, astronomy and moral philosophy. On many of these topics he wrote for the *Edinburgh Review* which he helped to found in 1802. Yet he never lost a fondness for fun that was a feature of his rather unruly youth and which did not always serve him well in later life.

Brougham was admitted as an advocate at the Scottish Bar in 1800 but, with his liberal views, he found little scope for his talents there and he travelled to London where he joined Lincoln's Inn on 14 November 1803. Five years later he was called to the English Bar. He soon allied himself with the Whigs centred on Holland House and he entered Parliament in 1810 where he carried a statute making participation in the slave trade a felony.

He first made a name for himself as a lawyer by his defence of the brothers John Hunt and John Leigh Hunt in two prosecutions for seditious libel in their newspaper, *The Examiner*. The first trial, on 22 January 1811, arose from an article entitled "One Thousand Lashes!!" which attacked flogging in the army. As William Cobbett had only recently been fined and sent to prison for two years for criticising army flogging in his *Political Register* the verdict against Hunt could hardly be in doubt.[1] Nevertheless, Brougham secured a brilliant acquittal and even the illiberal judge, Lord Ellenborough, after having summed up in favour of the prosecution, admitted that Brougham's speech was remarkable for "great ability, eloquence and manliness."

By contrast, in the second trial in 1812, he unsuccessfully defended the Hunts against the Prince Regent of whom they had written that he was,

> a violator of his word, a libertine, head over ears in debt and a disgrace as a despiser of domestic ties ... a man who had just closed half a century without one single claim on the gratitude of his country, or the respect of posterity.[2]

The Solicitor-General, Sir William Garrow, read the whole article to the jury in order that it might make its own effect[3] and, on this occasion, Lord Ellenborough, no doubt mindful of the rank of the prosecutor, said Brougham was "inoculated with all the poison of the libel".[4]

Nevertheless the trials secured his success as a barrister. Both comments of the judge, in fact, reveal different facets of Brougham's personality that were to surface time and again throughout his life. Despite his failings, however, he was always a dedicated campaigner for the causes of law reform, an extension of education, the abolition of slavery, Catholic emancipation, parliamentary reform and a free press. On the last he wrote that "even uproar is wholesome in England, while a whisper is fatal in France."[5]

Brougham was a fearless and energetic advocate although not entirely effective with juries. Although he steeped himself in the speeches of Cicero and Demosthenes his oratory was more suited to parliamentary debate where he excelled. His interest in, and knowledge of, literature and science

---

1. Robert Stewart (1986), *Henry Brougham: His Public Career—1778-1868*, London: The Bodley Head, p. 75.
2. *R. v. John and Leigh Hunt*, *The Times*, 10 December 1812, p. 1.
3. Trowbridge H Ford (1995), *Henry Brougham and his World: A Biography*, Chichester: Barry Rose, p. 181.
4. *The Law Magazine*, vol. 52. pp. 21-22.
5. Henry Brougham (1838), *Speeches*, Edinburgh, vol. 1. p. 15.

were deep and he had indomitable energy. On the other hand, he was often impulsive, excitable, wayward and capricious. As a consequence, he was widely distrusted by parliamentary colleagues and one of the nicknames coined for him was "Wicked Shifts".[6] However, his many positive qualities, despite his lack of settled principles, excited great admiration early in his career both in the country and the House of Commons.

Queen's Attorney-General

Under pressure from his parents, in 1795 the Prince of Wales, mocked as the "Prince of Pleasure", married Princess Caroline of Brunswick, on whom he had never set eyes. The couple hated each other from the beginning and before long the Prince sent his wife and her baby away. However, by 1820 the Princess was demanding to have her honour redeemed and to return to take her lawful place beside her husband. She had now become the darling of the people and Brougham and Samuel Whitbread were engaged to act as her legal advisers. Brougham used the opportunity to play politics although his devious behind-the-scenes manoeuvres caused consternation even among members of his own party. These were unknown to the general public, however, where his fame grew apace.

When George III died on 29 January 1820, the Prince became king as George IV and, seizing on a dossier prepared by Caroline's enemies alleging misconduct abroad with an Italian, he ordered the drawing up of a Bill of Pains and Penalties as a means to prosecute her for adultery. The Bill contained a clause to deprive Caroline of her title of queen and another to annul her marriage to the king. She, in response, appointed Brougham to act as her Attorney-General.

Prosecution of the Queen

The trial before the House of Lords was set for 17 August 1820. By now London was in a frenzy of delirious excitement and support for the Queen with huge crowds thronging the streets with flaring torches and filling craft upon the river. Shouts of "The Queen! The Queen!" rang out everywhere. In ale-houses toasts to the health of the king's enemies were drunk by soldiers

---

6. John Hostettler (1992), *The Politics of Criminal Law: Reform in the Nineteenth Century*, Chichester: Barry Rose Law Publishers, p. 34.

and the government began to fear bloody revolution. The trial was a purely political act and there was no necessity to prove guilt beyond a reasonable doubt as in a criminal trial. Brougham made a brilliant opening speech and his peroration pleading for mercy and justice for the queen led to Thomas Erskine rushing from the House in tears.

Brougham's Triumph

The proceedings were drawn out but eventually Brougham audaciously took the initiative by obliquely suggesting that he held in reserve the secret of the king's secret illegal marriage to Mrs Fitzherbert, the disclosure of which would have meant the king's abdication. Brougham then proceeded to tear to shreds the flimsy evidence of many prosecution witnesses. The nation rocked with laughter when witnesses from Italy, and in particular a trusted servant of the Queen named Theodore Majocchi, constantly replied to Brougham's penetrating questions with the words, *Querto non mi ricordo* (I do not remember). Referred to by *The Times* as "Signor Non Ricordo", Majocchi, and other witnesses who joined in the refrain, lost all credibility. Reluctantly, the government recognized that it was defeated and announced that it would not send the Bill to the House of Commons.

The Queen travelled in triumph to her home on the banks of the Thames near Hammersmith amidst tumultuous throngs of frenzied people. However, in keeping with his conduct throughout, the king prevented Caroline from attending his coronation in Westminster Abbey where she was rudely turned away at the door. His continuing dilemma was resolved, however, when she unexpectedly died on 7 August 1821. Brougham accompanied her body to Germany where she was buried in the family vault of her native Brunswick.

Contrary to what was generally expected when he undertook the case, as a result of his speech in defence of Caroline, Brougham's practice at the Bar increased substantially and the courts were crowded with people who came from far and wide to see and hear him. He was widely looked upon as the champion of the people and he also became recognised as the most formidable member of the Whig opposition in Parliament. Next to the king, wrote Macaulay, Brougham is the most popular man in England.

A Hatful of Oranges

On 7 February 1828, when MP for Winchelsea, Brougham made an eloquent speech on law reform pleading for "the pure, prompt and cheap administration of justice". This celebrated speech was the longest he ever made in the House of Commons and was delivered over six hours whilst he refreshed himself with oranges from the top hat beside him. He raised every field of jurisprudence and every type of court. He indicated defects and suggested remedies. He finished with a peroration that has rebounded ever since:

> It was the boast of Augustus ... that he found Rome of brick and left it of marble ... But how much nobler will be the Sovereign's boast when he shall have it to say that he found law dear, and left it cheap; found it a sealed book — left it a living letter; found it the patrimony of the rich — left it the inheritance of the poor; found it the two-edged sword of craft and oppression — left it the staff of honesty and the shield of innocence![7]

J B Atlay, in his book, *The Victorian Chancellors*, wrote of the speech that it led "to a greater number of beneficial and useful reforms than any other, ancient or modern".

Later, Brougham became MP for Yorkshire, the largest constituency in the country, and statesmen of the calibre of Canning and Peel declined to speak before him in the House for fear of his replies. However, when Lord Grey formed a Whig ministry in 1839 his colleagues were extremely apprehensive about Brougham's plans for parliamentary reform, as well as the possibility of his becoming prime minister, and they offered him the Great Seal.

Lord Chancellor

At first Brougham refused the offer of becoming Lord Chancellor. His mother wrote to him,

> Do not be tempted to leave the House of Commons. As Member for Yorkshire, backed by all you have done for the country, you are more powerful than any official that ever existed, however high in station or rank. Throw not away the

---

7. Robert Stewart. *Henry Brougham: His Public Career 1778-1868. Op. cit.* p. 237.

great position you have raised yourself to—a position greater than any that could be bestowed by King or Minister.[8]

But a Whig government could not be formed without him and friends told him that if he declined the office he could keep his party out of power for another 25 years and the country would lose all the good it could do. It is difficult to see the logic of this but Brougham weakened and accepted the Woolsack, to his everlasting regret. The king aptly summed up the position when, taking the credit, he told Lord Holland, "You are all under a great obligation to me. I have settled Brougham. He will not be dangerous any more."[9]

The Great Reform Act

Nonetheless, Brougham played a considerable part in securing the passage of the Great Reform Act of 1832 and was soon at the height of his fame. Many peers in the House of Lords opposed the Reform Bill which sought to abolish "rotten boroughs"[10] and introduce a fairer franchise than existed at the time. In a speech described by *The Times* as overpowering, matchless and immortal, Brougham, as Lord Chancellor, and sustained this time not by oranges but by mulled port, spoke for four hours and on bended knees exhorted the peers to accept the Bill. According to Lord Campbell in his *Lives of the Lord Chancellors,* Brougham, "continued for some time as if in prayer, but his friends, alarmed for him lest he should be suffering from the effects of the mulled port, picked him up and placed him safely on the Woolsack". Unfortunately the Lords rejected the Bill although in time they were persuaded to support it and it became law in 1832.

Law Reform

However, Brougham's career in office came to a swift end when the Ministry was dismissed by the king in 1834. On the other hand, his contribution to legislative reforms was to prove enduring. His great speech on law reform in

---

8. 2 Henry Brougham (1871), *The Life and Times of Henry, Lord Brougham,* London and Edinburgh: W Blackwood & Sons. vol. iii, p. 80.
9. Sir Denis Le Marchant Diary (30 November 1830). In Arthur Aspinall (ed.) (1952), *Three Early Nineteenth Century Diaries,* London: Williams & Norgate, p. 4.
10. A rotten or pocket borough was a constituency with a tiny electorate that could be used by a patron to gain unrepresentative and hence undemocratic influence in Parliament..

1828 produced useful reforms in the law of real property and in the practice and procedure of the Common Law courts. He secured the introduction of county courts and the formation of the Judicial Committee of the Privy Council. He supported the statutes which created the Central Criminal Court, reformed the Poor Law, abolished slavery and included many others too numerous to mention. He established the Law Amendment Society with its own journal, *The Law Review* in 1844 and throughout his life he kept the subject of law reform before the public.

In one of his last public appearances, at a dinner in the Middle Temple in 1864, Brougham referred to his speech on behalf of Queen Caroline and said that it was the duty of an advocate to reckon everything subordinate to the interests of his client. This earned him a rebuke from Lord Cockburn who replied that the arms which the advocate wielded were those of the warrior not the assassin. The incident led Atlay to comment,

> Poor Old Brougham! That was the light in which the budding Solicitor-General regarded the man who struck the fetters from the slave, who carried the Reform Bill in the teeth of King and Peers.[11]

In the end Brougham's mental powers began to decay and he died at Cannes on 7 May 1868 in his ninetieth year. A statue to him still stands in the French resort. And he should be remembered by his words in the peroration to his great speech on law reform in 1828 cited earlier.

---

11. J B Atlay (1906), *The Victorian Chancellors,* London: Smith Elder & Co., vol. i. pp. 375-6.

Chapter 7

John Adams
Constitutional Draftsman and President

Underestimated
To some extent John Adams has been airbrushed out of history as someone unequal to George Washington and Thomas Jefferson. Yet he was more single-minded in his determination to make secure the aims of the revolution once it had succeeded than in the power it brought. He was far more active than the other Founding Fathers of the USA and far more removed from the aristocrats of North America with their vast plantations and great numbers of slaves to which he never aspired. He also wrote on constitutional matters and persuaded Jefferson to lead the writing of the USA Declaration of Independence which Jefferson was too dilatory to undertake without the pressure Adams brought to bear on him. Jefferson was also a Francophile and totally anti-British whereas Adams was prepared to work with either country if it best suited the interests of the USA. Despite his worthy cold endurance in battle, Washington, for his part, was, after the success of the War of Independence, too much under the influence of the power-hungry Alexander Hamilton.

Enlightenment Values
John Adams was born on 19 October 1735 at Braintree (now Quincy) in New England in North America. His father, Deacon John Adams, was a farmer and his mother, Susanna Boylston came from a prominent Massachusetts family. He went to Harvard at the age of 16 and studied law in the office of

John Putnam a prominent lawyer at Worcester, Massachusetts. The colonists were still under British rule and his law reading included Sir Edward Coke's *Institutes* and Serjeant William Hawkins' *Pleas of the Crown*. Before long he became a lawyer himself in Boston as well as an outstanding statesman and political theorist. An Enlightenment figure he read Cicero, Tacitus, and others of his Roman heroes in Latin, and Plato and Thucydides in the original Greek. But in his need to fathom the "labyrinth of human nature", as he put it, "he was drawn to Shakespeare and Swift, and was likely to carry Cervantes or a volume of English poetry with him on his journeys".[1]

He distinguished himself at Harvard and was admitted to the Bar in Boston in 1759 at the age of 24. He attended courts in Boston to hear and learn from the example of the experienced advocates who were appearing there. He soon built up his own general practice, aided by a clear voice and a strong moral sense, and became the leading lawyer in Boston. At nearby Weymouth on 25 October 1764 he married Abigail Smith, his third cousin, and, being both intelligent and forthright, she was able to nurture his independent spirit throughout their married life. When they were in England, and experienced the hostility of the aristocratic court, they befriended the radical Richard Price and Mary Wollstonecraft who had a strong influence on Abigail. Also in London, in 1783, Adams lodged with the radical publisher John Stockdale who was later prosecuted by the House of Commons for publishing a book which compared the action of the House in its impeachment of Warren Hastings to an inquisition. Defended by Thomas Erskine (mentioned in the *Preface* and *Chapter 6*), Stockdale was found not guilty by a special jury.

Adams was an enthusiastic champion of independence from Great Britain and in 1775 he proposed the election of George Washington as commander-in-chief of the colonists' army and after victory in the War of Independence he served two terms as Washington's Vice-President. In 1796 he was himself elected as the second President of the USA. He practised Enlightenment values and was a Founding Father of that country and helped Thomas Jefferson to draft the Declaration of Independence in 1776.

---

1. David McCullough (2001). *John Adams*. New York, Simon & Schuster Paperbacks. p. 19.

The Boston Massacre

Adams had quickly made his mark as a lawyer and, early in his career, in 1770, he was asked to defend British soldiers charged with murder arising from what became known as the "Boston Massacre". This occurred at a time of intense tension in the city which led three years later to the Boston Tea Party in December 1773. As an enthusiast for independence from Britain he was reluctant to act for the soldiers since doing so might well do damage to his political reputation. However, as most of the other lawyers in Boston had been approached and had declined the defence, Adams considered that the principle that prisoners were deemed to be innocent unless found guilty by an independent jury after a fair trial meant that despite the difficulties he should in fact represent the soldiers.

Accordingly, he accepted the brief and in his opening words to the jury said,

> I am for the prisoners at the bar, and shall apologise for it only in the words of the Marquis Beccaria [who wrote] "If I can but be the instrument of preserving one life, his blessing and tears of transport shall be a sufficient consolation to me for the contempt of all mankind".[2]

It is interesting that Adams should use this sentiment from Cesare Beccaria's breathtaking book, *On Crimes and Punishments*, that had set European penal reform alight. And John Quincey Adams, his grandson and sixth USA President, was later to recall,

> the electrical effect produced upon the jury, and upon the immense and auditory, by the first sentence with which he opened his defence, which was a citation from the then recently published work of Beccaria.[3]

The so-called massacre initially arose from a number of youths snowballing a party of British army redcoats. However, soon, hundreds of people surrounded the Boston Custom House which was guarded by only one

---

2. Frederick Kidder (1870), *History of the Boston Massacre*, Albany, New York: Joel Munsell, p. 232.
3. Charles Francis Adams (1856), *The Works of John Adams, Second President of the United States, With a Life of the Author, Notes and Illustrations*, Boston: Little Brown, vol. ii. pp. 238-9.

British soldier until he was reinforced with eight others. Some men were then alleged to have attacked the soldiers with clubs and cudgels and caused many injuries. There were also cries of "Kill them! Kill them!" and one soldier was knocked down by a club and hit again before he could rise. It appears that in the confusion soldiers, without orders, fired their rifles, killing three youths outright and wounding others, two of whom died later.

A number of the soldiers were brought to court and in a trial that lasted for several days were charged with murder under the English Common Law of which Adams had an extensive grasp. A good many witnesses testified for both the prosecution and the defence and Adams argued that the evidence showed that in a riot the soldiers had only acted in self-defence when attacked. He cited well-known English jurists to show that mercy was a part of justice and declared that if there was any reasonable doubt in the minds of the jury of the prisoners' guilt they should declare them innocent—a principle that was not yet established in English law or any other legal system. Indeed, at the time, in cases of homicide once the killing had been proved the burden of proving their innocence rested upon accused persons. Adams told the jury that facts were stubborn things and whatever the feelings of passion they could not alter the state of facts and evidence.

In the event, there was no conclusive evidence that an order to fire had been given, or who fired the shots. As a consequence, after retiring for two hours, the jury found six of the soldiers not guilty, having acted in self-defence, and two were acquitted of murder but found guilty of manslaughter. The passage from Beccaria, spoken with passion by John Adams may have had a powerful effect on the jury. Clearly Adams' grandson thought so. And it is also clear that the soldiers benefitted from the advocacy of Adams in a city that would have had little sympathy for them. The fee paid to Adams was 18 guineas which was collected from the soldiers.

Not surprisingly, some antagonism towards Adams followed the trial and his practice fell off. And at this point he was offered the post of advocate-general in the Court of Admiralty but turned it down as being an office of the Crown. But notwithstanding some bad feeling, the Boston Town Meeting elected him as a representative to the Massachusetts legislature. He also quickly regained his reputation as a lawyer and appeared in over 200 Superior Court cases in one year.

More congenial to him than being appointed an officer of the Crown was his election to be one of the delegates from Massachusetts to the first and second Continental Congresses of the 13 colonies to be held in Philadelphia in 1774 and from 1775 to 1777. Here he was a powerhouse in the movement for independence although he experienced serious opposition in the harsh and bitter struggle to ensure unanimity among the representatives of all 13 states. It was here that, supported by Benjamin Franklin, he persuaded Thomas Jefferson to draft the Declaration of Independence which, again against stiff opposition, the Congress passed.

In Amsterdam

In 1777 and 1779 Adams was sent to France to seek help in the War of Independence with French soldiers and ships. However, receiving little assistance he proceeded to Holland in order to render America less dependent on the French government. Here he secured a huge loan of five million guilders from Dutch bankers and recognition of the new USA by the Dutch government. At a dinner in Amsterdam one day, Adams met a Mr Calkoen, a leading lawyer of that city. Calkoen sent Adams 29 questions about America and it is interesting to give a glimpse, by way of examples, of a few of the extensive replies Adams gave despite being so busy in affairs of state in wartime.[4]

Calkoen had asked, "Whether the common people in America are not inclined, nor would be able, to find sufficient means to frustrate by force the good intentions of the skilful politicians?" Adams replied that the commonalty had no need to have recourse to force in order to oppose the intentions of the skilful.

> The law and the constitution authorise the common people to choose governors and magistrates every year; so that they have it constantly in their power to leave out any politician, however skilful, whose principles, opinions, or systems they do not approve.

Another question was, "Are there no malcontents in America against the government, who are otherwise much inclined for the American cause, who

---
4. Charles Francis Adams (1852), *The Works of John Adams, Op. cit.* vol. vii, pp. 266-312.

may force the nation, or Congress, against their resolutions and interests, to conclude a peace?" Adams replied that,

> There is no party formed in any of the thirteen States against the new constitution, or any opposition against the government that I have ever heard of, excepting in Pennsylvania, and in North Carolina ... The party in Pennsylvania will never have an inclination to force the Congress, against their interests, to make peace; nor would they have the power, if they had the will. The party in North Carolina, whose inclination cannot be doubted, is too inconsiderable to do anything.

Calkoen then asked, "Do they who have lost their possessions and fortunes by the war, endure it patiently, as compatriots, so that nothing can be feared from them?" Losing fortunes in America, replied Adams, "has not such dreadful consequences, to individuals or families, as it has in Europe. The means of subsistence are easier to be obtained, so that nobody suffers for want." Those he knew, he said, had borne their losses with great fortitude and were determined to resist the more deplorable situation they would be in under the government of the English.

The 29th and last question was, "What are the real damages sustained, or still to be suffered, by the loss of Charleston? And what influence has it had on the minds of the people?" In reply, said Adams,

> An interruption of the commerce of indigo and rice; the loss of many negroes, who the English will steal from the plantations, and send to the West India islands for sale; a great deal of plunder of every sort; much unhappiness among the people; and several lives of very worthy men will be lost; but the climate will be the death to European troops, and, at an immense expense of men and money, they will ravage for a while, and then disappear. The effect of the surrender of Charleston, and the defeat of General Gates, has only been to awaken the people from their dreams of peace.

Constitution of Massachusetts
In October 1780, whilst the War of Independence was still in progress Adams was writing the state Constitution of Massachusetts which was, in his words, to provide for government of laws, and not of men. This guaranteed free

elections, freedom of speech and a free press. It provided against unreasonable searches and seizures and for trial by jury. The legislature, executive and judiciary were to be separate and Supreme Court judges to be appointed for life (subject to good behaviour). Nothing was said of slavery, it being considered by all parties as a divisive issue likely to undermine unity in the struggle for independence. But, it is significant that, unlike Washington and Jefferson, Adams never purchased a slave and never employed slave labour. Any blacks who worked for Abigail were free men. This Constitution of the Commonwealth of Massachusetts is the oldest functioning written constitution in the world.[5]

Paris and London

After Britain's defeat in the War of Independence at Yorktown, Adams was sent to Paris to negotiate with the former enemy where he signed a treaty of peace in 1783 by which the British Government acknowledged the USA to be composed of free, sovereign and independent states. It was an exciting moment for him. His revolutionary dream, and his hard work and skills, had helped give birth to a new nation.

Two years later he served as Minister to Great Britain for three years with some reservations about how he, from a poor farming background, was treated by London society. He persisted, however, as the representative of the USA and while in London he published his *Defence of the Constitution* of that country in which he set out his views on the separation of powers that he had incorporated into the Massachusetts Constitution.

President of the United States of America

Under Washington, Adams became Vice-President of the USA in 1789 and he and the President were both re-elected in 1793. It is believed that when he became Vice-President he would have preferred to be appointed Chief Justice of the Supreme Court of the USA. However, when Washington declined to stand for a third term in 1796 Adams was elected to succeed him as President. Whilst President, Adams appointed John Marshall to be

---
5. David McCullough. *John Adams. Op. cit.* p. 225.

Chief Justice of the Supreme Court where he served for 34 years as perhaps the greatest Chief Justice in American history.

   Adams served only one term as President as a consequence of unprincipled and bitter attacks from Jefferson's Republicans as well as from the dominant group in his own Federalist Party led by his relentless enemy Alexander Hamilton. Jefferson was more suave than Adams with his farming background yet took a party line to secure the presidency away from Adams. But it was Adams who always put the new nation before party. As a consequence, he greatly strengthened the USA army and navy during the undeclared war with France from 1798 to 1800. Indeed, in the face of furious opposition from Hamilton and his supporters he managed to secure peace with Napoleon although the Republicans took the credit and Adams lost the presidency. It is likely, however, that if war had broken out as Hamilton wished and he had controlled a large army the USA itself may have experienced a military dictatorship with untold consequences for itself and the world.

Retirement
There can be no doubt that being steeped in the law was of great assistance to Adams during his various employments at the head of the USA government. As were his enormous energy and his utter honesty. But, on ceasing to be President, he retired to his farm at Braintee where he greatly enjoyed being a farmer once more. He also restored his old relationship with Jefferson, despite Jefferson snubbing him during his two terms as President, and they carried on an enjoyable correspondence during their retirement. Curiously, both of them died on the same day—the Fourth of July in the year 1826. Adams was 90-years-old. His body was buried beside that of his beloved Abigail who had predeceased him on 28 November 1818. His grandson, John Quincy Adams, was destined to become the sixth President of the USA on 4 March 1825.

Chapter 8

Helena Kennedy
Parliament, Court and College

Inspirational

Helena Kennedy QC is one of the most distinguished lawyers and active public figures in Britain today. She has spent her professional life giving voice to those who have the least power within the system, championing civil liberties and promoting human rights. She is an inspirational woman who has an incredible record as an outstanding lawyer in many fields, particularly in criminal law. A list of her achievements, awards and qualifications is a wonder to perceive. Among so many other things she is a member of the World Bank Institute's External Advisory Council and on the Board of the British Museum.[1] She stepped down as Chair of the British Council in July 2004 having held the post for six years. She is Vice-President of the Association of Women Barristers and a patron of Liberty (formerly the National Council for Civil Liberties). She is a Fellow of the Royal Society of Arts and President of the National Children's Bureau.

Mansfield College

Helena Kennedy was born in Glasgow on 12 May 1950 and studied law at the Council of Legal Education in London. She is married to Iain Hutchison with whom she has a daughter and a son. In July 2011 she was elected Principal of Mansfield College, Oxford. Mansfield has a dissenting tradition,

---

1. http://ashacentre.org/index.php/about/inspirational women/item/280-helena-kennedy

providing education for those who were originally excluded from Oxford University. Established in 19th-century it was the first college for religious Nonconformists. Incredibly, in 2011 some 84.5 per cent of its students came from sixth-form colleges and comprehensive schools. In an interview with Simon Baker for the *Times Higher Education* Kennedy said that the college avoids the "terrible snobbery" of some institutions. She said, "I came to Oxford and discovered that the upper-middle-classes had got it clocked. Hard to get into Oxford? You get your kids to apply to do Classics or some obscure language, or get them to apply to do Theology, because they are the areas that Oxford wants to keep alive but which get too few applicants". Mansfield has said it is extremely proud of its new Principal.

On her election, Kennedy also said, "Education changed my life and I want the exhilaration of that for others". Indeed, her involvement in education has included being the first Chancellor of Oxford Brookes University and President of the School of Oriental and African Studies. The Helena Kennedy Foundation provides bursaries to help seriously disadvantaged students from further education institutions to enter higher education.

As Baroness Kennedy of the Shaws, of Cathcart in the City of Glasgow, she is a Labour member of the House of Lords where she has rebelled against her party more than any other Labour peer with a dissent rate of 33.3%. Yet she remains admired and trusted by her party and the House. She is leading barrister, a broadcaster and a Bencher of Gray's Inn. In her professional work, as a member of the Doughty Street Chambers in London, she is an expert in human rights law, civil liberties and constitutional issues. Indeed, she has received honours for her work on human rights from the French and Italian governments and has been awarded over 30 honorary doctorates. In France she was created a member of the *Académie Universelle des Cultures*, in 1999, and in Italy a *Cavalier di Gran Croce* (that country's highest honour) by the President of Italy, in 2004.[2] In the same year the French Prime Minister made her a *Commandeur dans l'Ordre des Palmes Academiques*.

---

2. http://www.doughty street.co.uk/barristers/helena_kennedy_qc.cfm

Prominent Trials

In Britain, apart from acting in many key trials, her involvement in organizations and bodies to help people in need is extensive. Prominent high profile cases with which she has been involved include the following:

The Brighton Bombing

On 12 October 1984 an attempt was made to assassinate Prime Minister Margaret Thatcher and her Cabinet when they were staying at the Grand Hotel in Brighton for the Conservative Party Conference. A bomb exploded in the hotel killing five people and injuring 34. A member of the Provisional Irish Republican Army, Patrick Magee, was charged with five counts of murder and was found guilty. He was sentenced to eight terms of life imprisonment but was released from prison after serving 14 years.

The Appeal of the Guildford Four

In 1974, a bomb exploded in the Horse and Groom public house in Guildford, Surrey leaving five people dead and 65 injured. In the hysteria which followed, the police arrested four Irish men who were tried before Mr Justice Donaldson and a jury. There was no evidence linking the men with the IRA and they had alibis. As an indication of the terror to which the defendants were subjected, Gerry Conlon, one of the innocent accused was to write,

> When they put me in a cell in the police station, there was no mattress or anywhere to sit. There was no glass in the windows, so flurries of snow were coming in. I was shivering. To make myself small I rolled into the foetal position. A policeman came into the cell with an Alsatian as I was lying on the floor naked. He loosened the lead and the dog leapt at me. Its teeth were not even an inch away from my face. He said, "Don't lie down again or I'll come back with the dog and take it off the leash".[3]

All the accused and notwithstanding, they were found guilty of murder in October 1975 and sentenced to life imprisonment. The judge expressed his regret that they had not been charged with treason for which capital

---

3. Gareth Peirce (2010), *Dispatches from the Dark Side: On Torture and the Death of Justice*, London, Verso.

punishment then still remained the penalty. However, the men were found guilty on the basis of confessions which they had retracted—but to no effect. In a later appeal to the Court of Appeal in 1989 it was established that the police had used intimidation, including threats to family members and torture to secure the confessions. They had lied in their evidence and had kept evidence helpful to the defence from their counsel. The convictions were quashed and all were released, but only after serving 15 years in prison that profoundly changed their personalities and harmed their future lives.

The Michael Bettaney Espionage Trial

This was heard at the Old Bailey in 1984 when Bettaney, who was an intelligence officer in the counter-espionage branch of MI5, was charged under section 1 of the Official Secrets Act 1911 with passing sensitive documents to the Soviet Embassy in London. A graduate of Oxford University, he had been vetted twice for disloyalty but declared loyal despite being known for his alleged admiration for Adolf Hitler and singing the Horst Wessel song in local pubs.[4] He was alleged to have taken home from MI5 secret documents which he turned over to KGB officer Oleg Gordievsky who turned out to be an MI6 agent. He was found guilty and sentenced to 23 years imprisonment. He was released in 1998.

The Kidnapping of Baby Abbie Humphries

Baby Abbie was abducted from the maternity wing at Queen's Medical Centre, Nottingham in July 1994 by 22-year-old Julie Kelley, who simply walked out of the hospital with Abbie in her arms. Abbie's father had handed her to Kelley who was dressed as a nurse. Police eventually found her after her kidnapping had lasted 17 days and, taken to court, she was put on probation and started a new life in the Midlands. Abbie's family emigrated to New Zealand when she was ten-years-old and of course she was too young to now remember what happened and knows only what her family have told her about the abduction.

---

4. Paul Foot (1989), "Whitehall Farce", *London Review of Books*.

The Bombing of the Israeli Embassy in London.
This occurred with a car bomb on 26 July 1994 when 20 people were injured. Although a woman was seen with a car outside the embassy in Kensington immediately prior to the bomb exploding, five Palestinians were arrested in January 1995. Almost two years later two of them, science graduates who were educated in the UK were found guilty at the Old Bailey of conspiracy to cause explosions and sentenced to 20 years' in prison. Conspiracy is a notorious "catch-all" offence and nobody was ever convicted of the bombing.

Television and Films
In the fields of television and journalism Kennedy has made an outstanding contribution. She created the BBC television series "Blind Justice" in 1987; presented the BBC's "Heart of the Matter" in the same year and "Raw Deal on Medical Negligence" in 1989. She also presented "The Trial of Lady Chatterley's Lover" in 1990, and "Time Gentlemen, Please" for BBC Scotland for which she won the Television Programme Award category of the 1994 Industrial Journalism Awards. In 1992, with Polly Bide, she made the film *Mothers Behind Bars* which exposed the large number of innocent children born in British prisons with mothers often being shackled. So powerful was the impact of the film that it brought about changes in penal policy in women's prisons.

Her book *Eve was Framed: Women and British Justice* has won awards and shows the inadequacies of the law in certain areas. In particular, it examines how the British legal system discriminates against, women, the Irish, immigrants, young people, blacks and gays. Another book, *Just Law* deals with the condition of Britain today and the changing face of British justice. It is a striking attack on Ministers and others endeavouring to undermine long-established historical safeguards for defendants including trial by jury and the necessity to find an accused person in a criminal trial guilty "beyond reasonable doubt" and not on the easier to satisfy "balance of probabilities".

Charter 88
Helena Kennedy was a founding member of Charter 88, the constitutional reform group set up in 1988 following concerns about the failure of some British institutions to engage with democracy. As the organization grew

substantially in numbers she chaired it with considerable input from 1992 to 1997. She called for the UK to embrace a written Constitution, devolution, electoral reform, a Bill of Rights, a Freedom of Information Act, reform of Parliament and of the judiciary. With others she played a key role in persuading New Labour to embrace this reform platform as a central plank of its 1998 election manifesto. This led to the incorporation into British law of the European Convention on Human Rights, and a whole range of constitutional reforms including reform of the House of Lords.

Is it ethical to break the law?
Speaking about the suffragettes Kennedy asked if it was ethical to break the law in certain circumstances? My argument would be, she said,

> that there are some times when in pursuit of human rights it is the only thing that people can do. As a lawyer I'm not supposed to say that, but I think there are occasions when the general public would agree, that somehow one has to stand up to be counted. Obviously there have to be limits of what we consider to be acceptable in terms of civil disobedience. There are some political acts which one would never condone, and grappling with the ethics of where it is appropriate and what is appropriate is difficult. The courage of these women [the suffragettes] was extraordinary, in that they were prepared to sacrifice their lives. Now of course today we have people who are also prepared to sacrifice their lives and one has to consider when and where that is appropriate. And I think most of us would say anything that involved harm to others would be unacceptable.[5]

---

5. Cited in Neil MacGregor (2011), *A History of the World in 100 Objects,* London: Allen Lane, pp. 624-25.

Chapter 9

Norman Birkett
One of the 'Great Advocates'

Norman Birkett KC had a brilliant reputation as defence counsel in numerous notable murder trials. He was also a Liberal Member of Parliament, a judge in the King's Bench Division of the High Court, a judge at the Nuremberg War Trials and a Lord Justice of Appeal.

Call to the Bar
Birkett was born in Ulverston, Lancashire on 6 September 1883 to Thomas Birkett, a draper, and his wife Agnes who died of tuberculosis in the year after he was born. After attending Barrow-in-Furness Grammar School and working as an apprentice in one of his father's drapery stores he applied to go to Emmanuel College, Cambridge but had to pass an entrance examination which involved spending three months learning Latin and Greek. He was then accepted by the university to study Theology, History and Law in October 1907. He was called to the Bar by the Inner Temple on 4 June 1913. Seven years later he was married to Ruth Nilsson, who worked for Cadbury's at Bournville, on 25 August 1920.

During World War I he was declared medically unfit as suffering from tuberculosis and this assisted his career as a barrister when so many young men at the Bar were called up for war service. In 1920 came a breakthrough when he acted as junior for the prosecution in what was known as the Green Bicycle Case, in which a young woman was killed by a bullet wound to the head. The defence was led by Edward Marshall Hall (*Chapter 17*) then at the height of his fame as a leading King's Counsel. Although Marshall Hall secured the acquittal of the man accused of the murder he was so impressed by Birkett's conduct of the prosecution that he offered him a place in his chambers.

King's Counsel

As an MP Birkett was entitled to be appointed as King's Counsel and he took the opportunity on 15 April 1924. Early in 1927 he appeared in a libel action that aroused great public interest. The case was *Wright v. Gladstone*. The plaintiff, Captain Peter Wright, was at the time a London journalist and the defendant was Viscount Gladstone son of William Ewart Gladstone who had been Prime Minister four times in Victorian Britain. Gladstone wrote a letter to Wright which said,

> Your garbage about Mr Gladstone in "Portraits and Criticisms" has come to my knowledge. You are a liar.
>
> Because you slander a dead man you are a coward.
>
> And because you think the public will accept invention from such as you, you are a fool.
>
> (Signed) Gladstone.

To ensure that Wright would bring an action for libel against him Gladstone sent copies of the letter to Wright's publishers and to the journal *The Nation*.

Wright had based his allegations against the Liberal leader upon Gladstone's declared interest in rescuing prostitutes from the dangers of their calling. This led to him talking to them in the streets at night and visiting them in their rooms. In his book of essays entitled *Portraits and Criticisms* Wright had written,

> Gladstone founded a great tradition, since observed by many of his followers and successors with such pious fidelity, in public to speak the language of the highest and strictest principle, and in private to pursue and possess every sort of woman.

Gladstone had been dead for 30 years and a statement libelling a dead person was not actionable in English courts. Hence the attempt of his son to make Wright take libel proceedings against him in which he could defend his father's reputation. As a staunch Liberal MP himself Birkett was only too pleased to take what amounted to the defence of his boyhood hero.

Gladstone then wrote to the Bath Club of which both he and Wright were members and described Wright as a foul fellow. In the event it was on this letter that Wright sued for damages for libel. Gladstone pleaded four defences. First, that the words complained of were not libellous and did not injure the character of the plaintiff. Secondly, privilege. Thirdly justification. Fourthly, fair comment. In the main, however, he relied upon the defence of justification.

The action came before Mr Justice Avory and a special jury in the King's Bench Division of the High Court on 27 January 1927 with Birkett leading for the defendant. The thrust of the plaintiff's case, said his counsel Mr Boyd Merriman, later Lord Merriman, was that Lord Gladstone's attack on Captain Wright was an attempt to curtail the right of free discussion which no filial piety could for a moment excuse.

In reply to cross-examination by Norman Birkett, Wright confirmed that he believed Gladstone had been unfaithful to his wife for 60 years. He agreed that if such a charge were made falsely it would be a foul charge. But, he added, the man making it would not necessarily be a foul man. Lord Gladstone, he said, used bad English "and I can't talk bad English to please you, you know". Birkett continued in a tone of withering sarcasm, "If a person made a foul charge against you or your dead father, what would you call him in your beautiful English"?

"I should call him intemperate," replied Wright to laughter in court.[1]

A responsible journalist, asked Birkett, would regard it as his duty to verify the facts before making a serious charge against anybody?

---

1. H Montgomery Hyde (1964), *Norman Birkett. The Life of Lord Birkett of Ulverston*, London, Hamish Hamilton, p. 186.

"Not if he thought he knew them, otherwise he could never write anything," replied the witness.

Wright admitted that in his book he had said that Lily Langtry was Gladstone's mistress. A few days later Birkett produced a telegram addressed to him from Monte Carlo which read, "Strongly repudiate slanderous accusations by Peter Wright. Lily Langtry". Further questions backed by reliable documents proved that Wright had on occasion given false information which he was now obliged to withdraw in court. He had relied, he said, upon statements by people who were now dead. Finally, after further severe cross-examination, Wright said that he regretted publication of what he had said about Gladstone.

Birkett's eloquent speech over two hours in opening the defence was devastating in its merciless exposure of Wright's evidence providing no facts to back his allegations. "It is shameful, shameful!" he cried. When he came to address the jury after the evidence of Lord Gladstone, Birkett pointed out that whereas his client had spoken of direct personal knowledge of his father, Captain Wright had spoken on hearsay and rumour which, in every matter where they could test it, had broken down hopelessly. At the end of the case the jury found for Lord Gladstone who wrote to thank Birkett for his masterly cross-examination. The jury added that they considered the high moral character of the late W E Gladstone had been completely vindicated.

Member of Parliament

Birkett had been elected Liberal MP for Nottingham East in the 1923 general election. His maiden speech followed a proposal by a Labour Member that state pensions should be paid to widows with children and wives whose husbands were unable to work through injury. Birkett supported the motion but went further and argued that pensions should also be given to unmarried mothers, deserted wives and divorced wives. Despite the warm support his speech received his success as a barrister grew rapidly and he found little time to appear in the House of Commons.[2]

He lost his seat in the Commons in the landslide election defeat of the Labour government in the same year following the publication of the

---

2. H Montgomery Hyde, *Norman Birkett. The Life of Lord Birkett of Ulverston. Op. cit*, London, Hamish Hamilton, p. 119.

fraudulent Zinoviev Letter which purported to come from Communist International and give instructions to the Communist Party in Britain to provoke disaffection in the army and greatly strengthened the Conservative vote. He did, however, secure re-election for Nottingham East on 31 May 1929. Labour became the Government and with a shortage of experienced Labour lawyers in Parliament the Prime Minister, Ramsay MacDonald offered Birkett the post of Solicitor-General if he would join the Labour Party. Unwilling to desert the Liberal Party, Birkett declined the offer. Subsequently, after the economic crisis of 1931 he was defeated in the election in October, ceased to be an MP and never returned to the House of Commons.

The Blazing Car Trial

In 1930, Birkett was involved in what became known as "The Blazing Car Murder" trial. The police had been called to a burning car near Northampton on Guy Fawkes night and found in the boot a body with a face so badly burnt that it was impossible to identify the man. With the number plate of the car undamaged, however, the police traced its owner who proved to be Alfred Arthur Rouse. He was arrested and appeared at Northampton Assizes on 26 January 1931 charged with the murder of an unknown man. The prosecutors were Birkett and Richard Elwes. Rouse did not help himself with statements to the police such as, "I'm responsible" and that the car engine had been off at the time of the fire and thus could not have started the fire accidentally. His defence was that he had given an unknown man a lift and he had asked him to take the can of petrol in the car to fill up the tank. Whilst he was at the side of the road urinating he heard a loud explosion and thinking the petrol tank would explode he ran away. In fact it was believed, although not proved, that he intended it to be thought that he was the dead man.

Birkett's cross-examination of Rouse and other witnesses was devastating and the jury took only 15 minutes to find Rouse guilty. After his appeal was rejected he did in fact admit he had committed the murder. The case was unusual in that the victim was never identified and Rouse was found guilty of the murder of a person unknown. He was executed at Bedford Gaol.

The Brighton Trunk Murder

In 1934, Birkett acted in the defence of Tony Mancini, a 26-year-old waiter, in the second of two Brighton trunk murders. The first case was never solved and nobody was ever arrested. However, subsequently, another woman, Violette Kaye, had disappeared and the police interviewed her boyfriend, Toni Mancini. He told them that he had broken with Violette and she had gone to Paris. On 14 May 1934, he moved his belongings from the house he had shared with her including a large trunk which was too heavy to move by hand. He also told a friend,

> What is the good of knocking a woman about with your fists? You only hurt yourself. You should hit her with a hammer same as I did and [chop] her up.

A hammerhead was later found in the rubbish at his old house and at his new home, in June, the police found Kaye's torso decomposing in the trunk. Mancini denied the murder and said that he had returned home to find her dead and, thinking that with his criminal record the police would not believe him, he had hidden the body in the trunk.

Birkett agreed to lead for the defence of Mancini when he was brought to trial before Mr Justice Branson at Lewes Assizes on 10 December 1934. During the trial he highlighted small flaws in the prosecution case and managed to introduce an element of doubt in the minds of the jurors. He also emphasised the affectionate nature of the relationship between Mancini and Kaye. By his cross-examination he further suggested that Violette might have died from morphine poisoning, or had fallen down the steps at the basement flat at 44 Park Crescent, where she had lived with Mancini, and fractured her skull. Moreover, in the witness box Mancini made a good impression when giving his evidence in reply to Birkett's questions. However, there was strong evidence that he had committed the murder including marks on Kaye's skull believed to be made by a hammer and blood on Mancini's clothes.

But what was the motive? The case for the Crown, said Birkett, was that Mancini took a hammer and killed Violette Kaye:

> I waited, he continued, to hear some suggestion when Mancini was in the witness box as to why he had done it. There has not been a word upon this vital question.

I submit that this vital omission in the case for the Crown destroys it. All the evidence before the death of Violette Kaye is that they were friendly, affectionate, had no quarrels or rows, no anger, no words of bitterness, no malice; none of those things which are concomitant with cruelty, or injury.[3]

Similarly, he added, with the morphine in her body. It was astounding that it was more than a medicinal dose that may have been a fatal dose but Mancini was not asked a single question about it. On the questions of motive and morphine, ought not the jury to say that they had not been satisfied beyond reasonable doubt?[4] Apparently they agreed since after deliberating for two-and-a-half-hours they returned a verdict of not guilty. It was said that this was Birkett's greatest triumph in a capital case. Subsequently, when he was dying, Mancini confessed to the murder.

More Sensational Trials

Birkett continued to be much in demand. In addition to those cases already mentioned, his briefs included that for the defence in the trial in 1926 of Harriet Crouch on a charge of murdering her husband; of Beatrice Pace who was alleged to have poisoned her husband; of Sarah Hearn charged with arsenic poisoning in 1931; and of Dr. Buck Ruxton who was found guilty of murdering his wife and their children's housemaid in September 1935. All these defendants were represented in court by Birkett and, except for Dr Ruxton, against whom the evidence was overwhelming, they were found not guilty of the charge of murder.

Other sensational criminal cases in which he appeared were those of Jackson Palmer, accused of manslaughter arising from an illegal abortion in 1928; Clarence Hatry, charged in an enormous fraud in 1930; Maundy Gregory involved in the infamous Lloyd George honours scandal; and the "Mayfair Playboys" charged with a high profile jewel robbery with violence. In civil actions he also appeared for Lady Mountbatten in her successful libel action against *The People* newspaper and for Wallis Simpson in the divorce case against her second husband that freed her to marry King Edward VIII.

---

3. *Ibid*, p. 414.
4. *Ibid.*

Judge and the Nuremberg Trials

Birkett loved his work at the Bar and, as we have seen, he appeared in numerous high profile and sensational cases. But eventually, on 11 November 1941, he agreed to give it up and be sworn in as a judge of the High Court. However, it may have been a mistake and he subsequently admitted that he missed the limelight of being a successful advocate. Although he was a popular judge he believed he was too weak in his judgments since he did not desire to hurt people's feelings. In 1943 he suffered from heart disease and pneumonia that greatly reduced his stamina but he did not retire from the Bench until the end of 1956. In the meantime his career took an important new turn.

In the summer of 1945, at the end of World War II, Birkett was appointed alternate judge at the Nuremberg Trials of Nazi war criminals in Germany. Geoffrey Lawrence was the main British judge. The trials, which laid the basis for future trials for crimes against humanity, lasted from 18 October 1945 until 30 September 1946 and Birkett played a significant role in the proceedings which were described as being impartial under the Rule of Law. When he returned to England at the conclusion of the trials he received no material acknowledgment of his important role in the proceedings although Geoffrey Lawrence was made a Baron. This led him into depression which lasted some months and this was only partially lifted when he was made a Privy Councillor in the 1947 Birthday Honours List.

After some delays, which he found inexplicable, he was appointed to the Court of Appeal on 2 October 1950. He was not happy there, however, finding the work unexciting and doubting whether he was having an impact on the law. It seems likely that he was less suited to the Bench than in the body of the court acting as an advocate. In 1958 he was made Baron Birkett of Ulverston and took his seat in the House of Lords. He was also granted a Doctorate of Law by the University of Cambridge where it was said that he was, "endowed with such a voice as Cicero declared to be the first requisite of an orator" and that "in our own time there has been no one more skilled in swaying the mind of a jury".[5] It was a fitting tribute to an extraordinary advocate.

---

5. *Ibid.* p. 568.

Chapter 10

Jeremy Bentham
Utility, Punishment and Law

Jeremy Bentham, a prolific thinker and writer, has had a profound and lasting effect on English criminal law. "The age of law reform and the age of Jeremy Bentham are one and the same", wrote Lord Henry Brougham (*Chapter 6*). Indeed, his thinking is still relevant today as Professor H L A Hart has been at pains to point out in his *Bentham and Demystification of the Law*.[1] And Lord Lloyd of Hampstead, in his *Introduction to Jurisprudence*,[2] has gone so far as to claim that Bentham is one of the creators of the modern welfare state.

Infant Prodigy

Bentham was born into a family of lawyers in Houndsditch, East London on 15 February 1748. Before long it became clear that he had a prodigious mind but a feeble, dwarfish body. To make matters worse he was brought up by a bullying father who saw him as an infant prodigy and, in effect, denied him a childhood. At the age of three, he was found seated at a desk reading Rapin's huge folio *History of England* with a lighted candle on each side of him. At six, he was reading *Telemachus*, the son of Odysseus and Penelope in Homer's *Odyssey*, which he took up as a novel but which he claimed turned him into a philosopher. At the age of seven he was sent to Westminster School, at 12 to Oxford and at 16 to Lincoln's Inn. He was called to the Bar

---

1. H L A Hart (1982), *Essays on Bentham. Studies in Jurisprudence and Political Theory*, Oxford: Clarendon Press, pp. 21-39.
2. Lord Lloyd of Hampstead (1979), *Introduction to Jurisprudence*, London: Stevens & Sons.

in 1769 but, being appalled by what he saw as a combination of malpractices and out-dated legal precedents, he quit the profession in order to "put an end to them rather than profit from them". He turned his hand to writing for what he believed was the benefit of the world and his published works run to nearly six million words.

Paternalism

This led him, following the example of Cesare Beccaria, to give birth to the Utilitarian philosophy with its principle of the greatest happiness of the greatest number, which means the approval or disapproval of every action whatsoever according to its tendency to augment or diminish personal happiness. And it applies not only to the actions of individuals, but also to every measure of civil government. The paradox is that it means emancipation through paternalism. In setting out this philosophy, Bentham started a powerful movement for reform and philanthropy which undoubtedly had considerable appeal to the representatives of the new middle-class of his time. When he was joined by James Mill, the spokesman of the middle-class, a new philosophical radicalism was born. Soon he was to encourage Samuel Romilly and Henry Brougham (*Chapter 6*) in law reform and turn his own inventive mind to the concept of a complete codification of the rules of government and law. His followers were inspired to a greater or lesser extent by his fervour for codification of the law—one of the many terms he invented.

Thus, in his *Codification Proposal*,[3] he sought to combine his authoritarian and democratic views in a complete system of law parallel to that of his proposed *Constitutional Code* for regulating the entire relations of government and governed. His influence was to pervade the movement for codification of the criminal law in England throughout the 19th-century. First, with the 1933 Criminal Law Commissioners and then through Mill and Thomas Babington Macaulay in India with his Penal Code. Finally, later in the century, he was championed by James Fitzjames Stephen with his efforts to codify English criminal law. Stephen put into practice Bentham's theory of codification when he was Law Member of the governing Council in India.

---

3. Jeremy Bentham (1968 edn.), *Codification Proposal Addressed to All Nations Professing Liberal Opinions. Works,* London: Athlone Press,. vol. iv. pp. 535-594.

It was about India that Bentham also wrote his important essay on *The Influence of Time and Place*.[4]

His was a seminal influence in a period which saw the birth of modern industry; the rise of the working-class and Methodism; the American War of Independence and the French Revolution; the publication of the *Wealth of Nations* and the impact of the ideas of Rousseau, Hume and Paine; the Clapham Sect and — on the day on which Bentham died — the enactment of the Great Reform Act of 1832.

Science of Law

With his disciples Bentham subjected the whole of English law and government to the most searching examination ever witnessed up until that time. He studied and exposed in great detail the obscurity of the law as it then was as well as its complexity and expense, its artificiality and irrationality. He despised the unwritten Common Law with its judicial law-making and set out to replace it with a science of law based on logic and clarity of expression. He believed that,

> Lawyers love unwritten law for the same reason that the Egyptian priest loved hieroglyphics [and] priests of all religions have loved their particular dogmas and mysteries. They are a source of power, reputation and fortune.[5]

However, the *Law Magazine*, although otherwise full of praise, took Bentham to task for describing the judges as liars and frauds, and likened examples of his style to "…the grinning faces and burlesque forms with which the monkish builders have studded our magnificent cathedrals".

Refashioning the Entire Legal System

Bentham knew there could be no government without law and he sought to rescue law from obscurity and what he saw as a mean and oppressive function. He, therefore, undertook the Herculean task of refashioning the entire legal system of England and, indeed, those of the whole world if it

---

4. Jeremy Bentham, *The Influence of Time and Place in Matters of Legislation. Works – Ibid.* vol. i, pp. 171-194.
5. *Rationale of Judicial Evidence, Works*, vol. vii.

would permit him, on new and scientific principles. And in the process, he helped found a new philosophy for the rising middle-class. His advocacy of the principle of Utility was to produce a widespread energy, even fury, for reform, the impact of which advanced the immense shift in society that came about during his lifetime and after.

However, the connection was not direct. As John Stuart Mill (1806-1873) was to say of Bentham:

> We do not mean that his writings caused the Reform Bill ... the changes which have been made, and the greater changes which will be made, in our institutions, are not the work of philosophers, but of the interests and instincts of large portions of society recently grown into strength. But Bentham gave voice to those interests and instincts: ... he is the great subversive thinker of his age and country.[6]

But in his attempts to demystify and clarify the criminal law, he also condemned many of the rules of evidence, such as the exclusion of hearsay evidence, that were designed to protect the accused. Nevertheless, numerous reforms of the criminal law which he advocated, either by trenchant criticism of existing rules or by positive proposals for new ones, have gradually been woven into the fabric of the law with substantially beneficial results.

Opposition to the Death Penalty

Bentham was in advance of most of his contemporaries in following Beccaria in being totally opposed to capital punishment. In his *Rationale of Punishment*[7], written in 1775 but first published in Paris in 1811 and in London only in 1830, Bentham claimed that the death penalty had the undesirable effect of producing sentiments of pity for the sufferer, with the spectators at the gallows sharing his ordeal. These bloody executions, he said,

> ...are the real causes of that deep-rooted antipathy that is felt against the laws and those by whom they are administered; an antipathy which tends to multiply offences by favouring the impunity of the guilty.

---

6. John Stuart Mill (August 1838), "Bentham", *London and Westminster Review*, p. 469.
7. Jeremy Bentham (1830), *Works*, London: Athlone Press. pp. 1-143.

Such threatened fate, he claimed, also hardened criminals to the feelings of others as well as to their own feelings, and they saw every barbarity they inflicted as a justified reprisal. Since, at the time, death by hanging could follow for many trivial offences, such as stealing a handkerchief, or (a starving person) stealing food worth as little as a shilling, Bentham also saw the fairly frequent resulting leniency of judges and juries as harmful in bringing the law into contempt.

The desirable penal qualities lacking in capital punishment were described by him as follows:

1. The punishment of death could not be used for compensation since its source was destroyed.
2. Executed men could not be reformed and rendered of some use to society.
3. The death penalty was unequal since men were unequal. Death was the absence of all pleasure but also of all pain, and Bentham believed that many offenders would calculate the balance of each and consider life not worth keeping without the pleasures they could secure only by crime.
   In such cases punishment of death could be of no use. To this had to be added the criminal's calculation that infliction of the death penalty was by no means certain, and was distant compared with the existing discontent at not possessing the object of his passion.
4. A man might offend by a single and sudden act, oblivious to the prospect of pain to which he was subjecting himself. The death penalty was not variable and the amount of evil could not be increased or reduced.
5. Equally it was not remissible. This was important as judges were not infallible and many innocent victims had perished.

Analysis of Punishment

In his *Rationale of Punishment,* Bentham argued that all punishment was itself an evil. It was a kind of "counter-crime" committed with the authority of the law. But, upon the principle of Utility it was to be permitted in so far as it promised to exclude some greater evil. In fact, in this book Bentham analysed the whole subject of punishment in a scientific manner for the first time in history. Samuel Romilly said of it that, "penal legislation hitherto has resembled what the science of physic must have been when physicians did not know the properties and effects of the medicines they administered".

To Bentham, as with Beccaria (*Chapter 20*), the vital purpose of punishment was to protect society and not to inflict torments on the offender. He was totally opposed to transportation which he considered was unequal in its effect on different individuals. It also had little deterrent value by example to others and was wasteful of both lives and money. After rotting in the hulks for a year or two, he declared, a miserable wretch was crammed with hundreds of others into a floating prison in which he faced the risks of famine, disease and death, only to reach a life of slavery, suffering and misery. In its place he wanted to see three different kinds of imprisonment adapted for prisoners who had committed offences of differing degrees of seriousness. This meant simple detention for insolvents, penitentiary confinement for the reformation of offenders whose imprisonment was to be temporary and perpetual imprisonment for those who should never mix in society again.

New Type of Prison

Bentham had long been concerned about prison reform. He studied the work and ideas of the great prison reformer, John Howard, and considered his writings on prisons, "supplied a rich fund of materials, but that a quarry was not a house".[8] He was deeply interested in the punishment of imprisonment, which was very little used at the time, and began to ask himself whether its use could be extended as a secondary punishment by making it more effective, more humane and, at the same time, cheaper. His over-active mind now conjured up a novel type of prison to be called the Panopticon or "Inspection House".[9] In March 1792 he laid a proposal before Parliament to undertake the custody of 1,000 convicts in such a prison. Parliament approved the scheme and passed an Act two years later which adopted it.[10] The prison was to be distinguished by three striking new features.

---

8. C Phillipson (1923), *Three Criminal Law Reformers. Beccaria, Bentham, Romilly*, London: J M Dent & Sons Limited, p. 127.
9. Jeremy Bentham (1791), *Panopticon or The Inspection House. The Works of Jeremy Bentham*, Edinburgh: John Bowring, vol. iv. p. 37.
10. 34 Geo. 3, c. 84.

- Firstly, from the form of the building, a circular iron and glass cage of open cells, the governor would be able to see each prisoner (and gaoler) at all times without being seen by them and could give them orders without leaving his central inspection tower. "The spider in his web!" exclaimed Edmund Burke of such a governor[11] but the scheme was approved by both Charles James Fox and William Pitt.
- Secondly, the management of the prison was to be exercised under contract. The government would pay a fixed sum for the total expense of each convict, who would work in his cell for as long as 16 hours a day, and, in return, the contractor would have his profit after a proportion had been paid to the prisoner. This would replace the then existing system of fees paid to gaolers by prisoners.
- Thirdly, all accounts would be available for public inspection and the prison would be open at all times to every magistrate, and at certain hours to the public generally.

The cost factor for the scheme was of primary importance. Parliamentary reports had estimated that transportation was costing over one million pounds every ten years, approximately £38 for each convict. Under Bentham's contract, he calculated that each convict would cost the government a mere 13 shillings and ten pence, including one shilling and ten pence for the building and land. Also included would be a fund to indemnify persons injured in the course of the convicts' crimes.

Bentham saw the Panopticon as a civilising influence on society. Morals would be reformed, health preserved, industry invigorated, public burdens lightened, economy seated on a rock, the Gordian Knot of the Poor Law not cut but untied—all, he said, by a simple idea in architecture. More recently critics have accused Bentham, John Howard and Elizabeth Fry of desiring to control prisoners' minds with "machines for grinding men good". And although Parliament agreed to Bentham's cyclopic monster in 1794, it was never built at the Millbank site purchased for it where the Tate Britain Gallery now stands, or elsewhere in the UK. One was built in the USA and another at Breda in Holland, which still exists. Bentham was eventually

---

11. Gertrude Himmelfarb (1968), "The Haunted House of Jeremy Bentham" in *Victorian Minds*, London: Weidenfeld & Nicolson.

paid £23,000 in compensation by Parliament for his efforts in working on the project for many years, but he never lost the bitterness he experienced from the ultimate rejection of his scheme, due to its non-implementation and the many wasted years involved.

On imprisonment generally, Bentham saw some disadvantages but thought it perfect in regard to disablement, eminently divisible in duration and very susceptible to different degrees of severity. Whilst prisoners were not seen, which did not help to deter others, the prison itself was visible and might well strike terror in the beholder. Indeed, he went on to suggest that prisons which held medium-term and long-term offenders should exhibit on the outside various figures such as a monkey, a fox and a tiger to represent mischief, cunning and rapacity. Inside, should be placed two skeletons to represent the abode of death. All these devices indicate how clearly impressed Bentham was with the utility of visual aids.

Assessment

Bentham was a brilliant progeny of the Enlightenment but his work suffered from some serious defects. His overriding desire to see the whole of the law codified has proved unattainable, at least in England, despite the valiant work of the 1933 Criminal Law Commission and, later in the 19th-century, of Sir James Fitzjames Stephen. Furthermore, the pursuit of happiness, which meant abundance, equality and security, predominated in his plans over the pursuit of justice and prevention of cruelty. His elimination of motive took all meaning out of morality. And he failed to see criminals as complicated human beings.

Nevertheless, his influence on law reform was far-reaching throughout the 19th-century—the century of law reform. And, although only a glimpse of his formidable volume of work has been possible here, he remains a serious intellectual force for any critique of the English legal system. Of course, genius is always controversial but on law perhaps a Victorian perception of Bentham's achievement is best summed up by John Stuart Mill. He wrote that Bentham expelled mysticism from the philosophy of law and set an example in viewing laws in a practical light, as a means to certain definite and precise ends; that Bentham cleared up the confusion and vagueness attaching to the idea of law in general, to the idea of a body of laws; that he took a systematic view of the needs of society for which his criminal code was to provide and that he found the philosophy of judicial procedure in a more wretched state than even any other part of the philosophy of law and carried it at once almost to perfection. Even Mill, however, had to concede that the underlying concept of morality was missing.

Although Bentham's grandiose schemes were never accepted in full he inspired the more practical minds of Romilly, Peel, Brougham and various Criminal Law Commissioners to give effect to bringing our criminal law out of its dark medieval past into the modern world. Moreover, his brilliance and his output were overwhelming and as Sydney Smith wrote of him:

> Neither gods, men nor booksellers can doubt the necessity of a middleman between Mr Bentham and the public. Mr Bentham is long: Mr Bentham is occasionally involved and obscure: Mr Bentham invents new and alarming expressions: Mr Bentham loves division and subdivision, and he loves method itself more than its consequences. Those only therefore who know his originality, his knowledge, his vigour and his boldness, will recur to the works themselves. The great mass of readers will not purchase improvement at so dear a rate but will choose rather to become acquainted with Mr Bentham through the medium of the reviews—after that eminent philosopher has been washed, trimmed, shaved and forced into clean linen.[12]

---

12. Sydney Smith (1825), "Bentham's Book of Fallacies", *Edinburgh Review*, vol. xiii, p. 367.

Chapter 11

Geoffrey Robertson
Rights, Romans and Regicides

Human Rights

Geoffrey Robertson QC is a modern human rights and civil liberties lawyer who was born in Sydney, Australia on 30 September 1946. His education was at Sydney Law School where he obtained his law degree and won a Rhodes Scholarship to the University of Oxford where he graduated with the degree of Bachelor of Civil Law.[1] In 2006 he was awarded an honorary degree of Doctor of Laws by the University of Sydney. He was called to the Bar by Middle Temple in 1973 and became Queen's Counsel in 1988. After a friendship with Nigella Lawson he married the author Kathy Lette in 1990 and lives in London with her and their children.

He has appeared as leading counsel in fighting for justice in over 200 reported cases, many of them landmark cases in constitutional and criminal law. A large number of them have been in the European Court of Human Rights in Strasbourg and the Privy Council and House of Lords (now the Supreme Court) in London. He is widely known in courts throughout Britain and the Commonwealth as well as Hong Kong and Florida. Justice, he argues, is to be found in rules which provide for the possibility of beating the state at its own game — hence the title of one of his best-selling books, *The Justice Game* (1998).[2]

---

1. *Who's Who* (2010), P. 1960.
2. Geoffrey Robertson (1998), *The Justice Game*, London: Chatto & Windus.

Robertson developed a *pro bono* practice defending at the Privy Council men and women condemned to death in Commonwealth courts. He served part-time as a United Nations appeal judge at its war crimes court in Sierra Leone until 2007 and, in 2008, he was appointed by the UN Secretary General to be one of three distinguished members of the United Nations Internal Justice Council.[3] He is founder and head of Doughty Street Chambers, the leading human rights practice in the United Kingdom, is a Bencher of the Middle Temple and a Recorder in London. As if all this would not be more than enough work for most barristers and silks he is Visiting Professor in Human Rights Law at Queen Mary, University of London and has had visiting professorships at the Universities of Warwick and New South Wales. He also finds time to write books and numerous articles for journals such as the *New Statesman* and *Newsweek* and also for newspapers including *The Guardian, The Times, The Independent* and *The Daily Mail*. In these, as indeed in all his writings, he flourishes as a controversialist.

Blasphemy

As with other famous lawyers, from Robertson's many cases only a few can be referred to here. One early case was *Mary Whitehouse v. Denis Lemon and Gay News* in July 1977 — a private prosecution brought under the blasphemy law.[4] For the defendants, John Mortimer QC appeared for Lemon the publisher of the paper and Robertson for *Gay News*. Mrs Whitehouse was the self-appointed protector of the morals of the nation and she considered that homosexuality was abnormal sexual behaviour. During the trial at the Old Bailey she held prayer meetings in the corridors of the court urging divine intervention in the jury's deliberations. "A novel form of contempt of court," observed Robertson.

Gay News had published a poem by Professor James Kirkup, an established poet and playwright whose play called *Upon This Rock* had been performed in Peterborough Cathedral. In the poem he depicted Jesus as a gay outcast. In a nod to Oscar Wilde the poem was entitled, "The Love that Dares to Speak its Name". Mrs Whitehouse presented to the court an affidavit from an evangelical theologian who claimed the poem undermined three fundamental

---

3. Geoffrey Robertson Website (2009). www.geoffreyrobertson.com/index.html
4. See Geoffey Robertson QC, *The Justice Game, Op. cit.* pp. 135-61.

Anglican tenets, namely that Christ was without sin, that homosexuality is evil and that there cannot be sex in Paradise. John Smythe, prosecuting counsel, described the poem as "so vile it would be hard for the most perverted imagination to conjure up anything worse" but Bernard Levin and Margaret Drabble gave evidence that *Gay News* was a serious and responsible newspaper. Robertson and Mortimer did their best against hostility from the judge who virtually summed up in favour of the prosecution and the jury found the defendants guilty by a majority of ten to two. Appeals to the Court of Appeal and the House of Lords failed but *Gay News* flourished with its circulation rising from 8,000 to 40,000 and literature for and about homosexuals became commonplace. Another unintended consequence of the prosecution was that blasphemy law has been pronounced obsolete.

The Romans in Britain

This was the first play to be prosecuted in Britain. Written by Howard Brenton, a dramatist of world standing it was performed at the National Theatre in 1981 and depicted what Mary Whitehouse described as "Three Roman soldiers tearing off all their clothes and raping three young, male Britons in full view of the audience!" Although she had not seen the play or ever attended the National Theatre she demanded that the Attorney-General, Sir Michael Havers, prosecute the theatre for obscenity, but he declined to do so. She, therefore, decided to mount another private prosecution herself in the role of what Robertson described as the "Director of Private Prosecutions".[5] It meant she had to prove that the performance tended to deprave or corrupt and had no serious dramatic merit. The play's director, Michael Bogdanov who had won many awards, was accordingly charged with having procured an act of gross indecency between one male actor and another.

Robertson claimed that the play was not erotic, with the scene in question intended to terrify, not titillate, dealing, as it did, with an army of occupation and was meant to draw parallels with certain situations then existing in Northern Ireland and Africa. The trial came on in Court No.1 at the Old Bailey in March 1982 with Robertson being led by Jeremy Hutchinson QC. The prosecution was effectively defeated when the solicitor for Mrs Whitehouse,

---

5. Geoffrey Robertson QC (1999), *The Justice Game, Op. cit*, p. 166.

Graham Ross-Cornes, the chief witness against Bogdanov, revealed under cross-examination that he had been sitting in the gods of the theatre, ninety yards from the stage, when he saw what he claimed to be a penis. Jeremy Hutchinson QC, who led for the defence, exploded in ridicule.

"The back row!", he exclaimed, "you sat in the back row! The cheapest seats in the house—Mrs Whitehouse couldn't afford the front stalls? You go to this theatre, knowing your task is to collect evidence for a *very serious prosecution* of my client, a man who has never committed a single offence in his life, on a *very nasty* charge and you *sit in the back row?*" (Italics supplied).

Furthermore, Hutchinson demonstrated with great dramatic effect in the use of his thumb that Ross-Cornes could have witnessed the actor's thumb protruding from his fist and not a penis.[6]

After earlier denying Robertson's request that the Attorney-General enter a *nolle prosequi* (i.e. to take over the case and then end it) Sir Michael Havers now did just that and the crusade of Mrs Whitehouse was defeated.

Regina v. Boggs

In 1987 a young American artist, Stephen Boggs, was on trial in Court No.1 of the Old Bailey before Mr Justice MacNeill and a jury.[7] What was his crime? He was charged with reproducing a £10 British banknote contrary to section 18 of the Forgery and Counterfeiting Act of 1981. The work stood in the courtroom and appeared to resemble the original although it was signed "JSG Boggs" instead of Robin Leigh Pemberton. Furthermore, the portrait of Queen Elizabeth II was different from that on a real £10 note and whereas a banknote has two sides the painting had only one side. In addition, a banknote is a three-dimensional physical object used to make purchases, whilst the picture was meant to be looked at on a wall. So the apparent resemblance was false. One of the complaints of the Bank of England was that Boggs had not sought its permission to paint a banknote. But when Boggs apologised it also pointed out that artwork reproducing a banknote for the purpose of seeking the bank's consent was itself an offence under section 18(1). A truly Catch 22 situation. An artist could not draw the

---

6. *Ibid.* pp. 177-8.
7. *Ibid.* pp. 262-281.

currency without the bank's consent, and he could not obtain that consent without submitting a drawing.

Robertson appeared for the defence. Addressing the jury he said,

> When Van Gogh, that anguished and tormented artist, painted a picture of irises, he could have had no idea that in 1987 his picture would be sold for £25 million to Alan Bond. A life-size photograph, a true "reproduction", can be bought for a few pounds. So can real irises. For £25 million you could have thousands of real irises delivered every day for the rest of your life. The Bank of England would say, "Oh, that Van Gogh original is a reproduction of the irises growing in a field in the South of France in the spring of 1876". The art critic might say the picture is not about irises at all, it's about human anguish, about rage against the squalor and shortness of our life compared with the eternal beauty and refulgence of nature ... What is Boggs saying, when he talks like Van Gogh of "bleeding into his pictures"?

Boggs had said this while being interviewed by police officers under caution. He had been arrested by a flying squad of senior detectives who burst into the gallery where the painting was being exhibited and seized his work. During questioning at Southwark Police Station by a Chief Inspector, he had remarked that he had "bled on to this piece of work".

Robertson persuaded Robert Hughes, art critic of *Time* magazine to provide a witness statement in which he made a distinction between "reproduction" (exact copying to produce a facsimile of the original) and "representation" (making a picture of a subject). He wrote:

> If I sit down with my watercolours and draw a tree, I am representing it. Nobody is expected to compare my drawing with a real tree, although (if I am lucky) there may be people who admire the fidelity and truth with which I have represented the tree—the way its branches go, the colour of the leaves and so forth. This simple distinction will, I hope, clarify the nature of what Boggs has been doing in these works. The Bank of England is putting itself in the position of the silly bird which, in Pliny's story, flew down and pecked at a bunch of grapes painted by Zeuxis, believing them to be the real thing.

The prosecution had believed they were presenting the jury with an open-and-shut case claiming that an artist could not expect to be above the law. Robertson responded by indicating that as Boggs himself had said to the police, a picture of a horse may have all the features of a horse but you don't saddle it. In his summing-up to the jury the judge said the case had nothing to do with art and declared that each of the defence arguments were utterly without merit. Yet, after retiring for less than ten minutes, the jury returned to declare Boggs not guilty. For his part the judge turned to the prosecuting counsel and whispered, "Well, Mr Harman, you learn something new every day".

Salman Rushdie

Robertson has appeared many times before the European Court of Human Rights and in various courts across the globe. His struggle for justice involved him in the defence of Michael X on death row in Trinidad convicted of murder[8] and Vaclav Havel in Communist Prague. Then, when, in 1989, Ayatollah Khomeini issued a *fatwah* to have the author Salman Rushdie killed for publishing his novel *The Satanic Verses*, Robertson, no doubt at some risk to himself, gave sanctuary in his home to Rushdie. When some Muslims attempted to flush him out by asking a Bow Street magistrate to order Rushdie to attend a private prosecution for blasphemous libel the magistrate refused on the ground that the crime of blasphemy only related to offences against the Christian religion. On the appeal to the High Court, Robertson represented Rushdie against 13 Muslim barristers who appeared for the prosecution. Death threats were made against the judge, Lord Justice Tasker Watkins VC and defence counsel but the trial continued.

Robertson studied the Koran and reached the conclusion that even if the law of blasphemy had covered Islam *The Satanic Verses* still would not have infringed it. This was also the view of the court and the government announced that it would not extend blasphemy to cover other religions or invoke it for divisive and damaging litigation, thus ensuring that there would be no future prosecutions for blasphemy by the state.

---

8. Formerly Michael De Freitas and Michael Abdul, Michael X was hanged in Trinidad in 1974.

The Tyrannicide Brief

John Cooke was the barrister who, in 1649, prosecuted King Charles I in the treason trial that led to the King's execution. Yet, until the publication of Robertson's biography of him in 2005,[9] little was known about Cooke who had been more or less airbrushed out of history. The son of a poor Leicestershire farmer, Cooke's love of liberty gave him the courage to bring the King to justice which led to the sovereignty of Parliament and England's only period as a Republic. He was appointed Solicitor-General to conduct the trial when more senior lawyers fled London or pleaded illness to avoid being associated with the trial. Charles refusing to recognise the court, declined to plead to the charge of treason but Cooke argued that in cases of treason a refusal to plead was taken as a confession of guilt. The court so held and after the court heard evidence for the prosecution Charles was found guilty and beheaded outside the Banqueting Hall in Whitehall. However, Cooke also paid with his life following the Restoration to the throne of Charles II — for making tyranny a crime.

John Cooke is associated with John Lilburne in originating the right to silence of the accused and he encouraged lawyers to accept a duty to act free of charge for the poor. Oliver Cromwell appointed him as a reforming Chief Justice in Ireland, but in 1660 he was brought before the Old Bailey in London where he was tried in a poisoned atmosphere with prosecuting counsel prepared to lie about what Cooke had said in the trial of the King. A witness gave perjured testimony and prosecuting counsel browbeat the jury. Cooke argued that he had only done his duty to act according to his brief as counsel in the King's trial and had only asked the court to do justice. However, under heavy pressure the jury found him guilty and he was brutally executed. Nevertheless, he had conducted the first trial of a head of state for waging war on his own people for which he is a lasting inspiration to the modern world.

Robertson has also been on several human rights missions on behalf of Amnesty International. Countries involved have included Vietnam, South Africa, Czechoslovakia, Malawi and Mozambique. His work on human

---

9. Geoffrey Robertson QC (2005), *The Tyrannicide Brief: The Story of the Man who sent Charles I to the Scaffold*, London: Chatto & Windus.

rights and civil liberties across the globe is an inspiration to all, inside and outside of the law.

Chapter 12

Abraham Lincoln
Law, Politics and Civil War

Rule of Law

Although a lawyer by profession, Abraham Lincoln is best known as the man who destroyed slavery in the USA. This represented a decisive step in the history of North America despite the fact that it was achieved in the course of his struggle to maintain the Federal Union. Abolition of slavery was not his primary purpose. Nevertheless, he deplored slavery and saw the Union as a means to securing freedom for the slaves. He strongly believed that America was a country under the Rule of Law. With the law, the USA was everything: without the law it was nothing.[1]

Lincoln was a humble and gawky man who was described by Walt Whitman as perfectly composed and cool with

> his unusual and uncouth height, his dress of complete black, stovepipe hat pushed back on the head, dark-brown complexion, seam'd and wrinkled yet canny-looking face, black bushy head of hair, disproportionately long neck and his hands held behind him as he stood observing the people.[2]

It brings to mind a familiar picture of the man who became the Republican President in November 1860 despite being described by the Democratic press as a third-rate lawyer. He then led the North to victory in the great

---
1. Paul Johnson (1997), *A History of the American People,* London: Weidenfeld & Nicolson, p. 190.
2. Cited by Paul Johnson, *A History of the American People, Op. cit,* p. 404.

constitutional, military and moral crisis of the American Civil War. But when he was needed to persuade Congress to avoid revenge and show compassion to the defeated Confederacy he was assassinated by a Confederate sympathiser in 1865. Here were all the ingredients to make him the popular folk-hero he became.

Law and Politics

Lincoln was born in a one-room log cabin in Hardin County, Kentucky on 12 February 1809. His grandfather, also Abraham, had been killed in an Indian ambush in 1786 with his children, including Lincoln's father, Thomas, looking on. Later, when an adult, Thomas was a restless pioneer but became well-known and well-liked in Kentucky and was reasonably wealthy until 1816 when he lost all his land in court cases because of faulty property titles.[3] As a consequence, Abraham as a young man lived in relative poverty. He received little formal education from a few itinerant teachers and was mostly self-educated.

In 1832, Lincoln was living in New Salem, Illinois where he decided to become a lawyer. He taught himself law by reading Blackstone's prestigious *Commentaries on the Laws of England* and other legal works. He was admitted to the Bar in 1836 and moved to Springfield, Illinois where he began to practise. Two years prior to that he was elected to the Illinois House of Representatives where he served for four terms as a Whig. Thus, his interest in the law and in politics were intertwined early in his career. On 4 November 1842, he married Mary Todd who was from a wealthy slave-owning family.

As a legislator, he voted to expand the suffrage to all white males in the state not just those who were owners of land. At the same time on the issue of slavery he said the, "Institution of slavery is founded on both injustice and bad policy, but the promulgation of abolition doctrines tends rather to increase than abate its evils".[4]

As a lawyer he became very successful and was considered a formidable advocate. In Springfield he undertook every kind of business that came his way and described himself as a "prairie lawyer". During the country's western expansion he handled many transportation cases which often dealt with

---

3. Carl Sandburg (1926), *Abraham Lincoln. The Prairie Years:* London: Jonathan Cape, p. 20.
4. David Herbert Donald (1995), *Lincoln*, London: Cape, p. 134.

conflicts arising from the operation of river barges under new railway bridges. As his reputation grew he appeared before the Supreme Court to argue an important case involving a canal boat that sank after hitting a bridge.[5] In another case he represented the Alton and Sangamon Railway in the Illinois Supreme Court in a dispute with James Barret one of its shareholders. Barret refused to pay the balance to buy his shares in the railway on the grounds that the company had changed its original train route. Lincoln successfully argued that the company was not bound by its original charter that was in existence at the time Barret agreed to pay for his shares. The charter, he said, had been amended in the public interest to provide a newer, superior and less expensive route, and the company retained the right to demand Barret's payment.[6] He appeared before the Supreme Court in 175 cases, in 51 of them as sole counsel, of which 31 were decided in his favour.

Murder Trials

Lincoln's most famous criminal defence was that of William "Duff" Armstrong at his trial in 1858 for the murder of James Metzker. During the trial Lincoln used a fact established by judicial notice to challenge the credibility of an eyewitness. After a prosecution witness testified to seeing the crime in the moonlight, Lincoln produced a *Farmers' Almanac* to show that at the time of the killing the moon was at a low angle which drastically reduced visibility. On the basis of this evidence, Armstrong was acquitted. In a case a year later Lincoln was defending his cousin, Peachy Harrison, against a charge of stabbing another person to death. Unusually for him, Lincoln angrily protested at the decision of the judge to exclude evidence favourable to the defendant. It was expected that Lincoln would be held in contempt of court but instead the judge reversed his ruling and Harrison was acquitted.

Republican Politics

Lincoln disapproved of slavery and its spread to new USA territory in the west. Accordingly he opposed the pro-slavery Kansas-Nebraska Act of 1854 which gave to settlers the right to determine whether to allow slavery in their new territories. Lincoln believed the decision should be made by Congress

---

5. *Ibid*, pp. 156-7.
6. *Ibid*, p. 155.

which had a duty to uphold the equality of all men as expressed in the Declaration of Independence. At this stage he was opposed to the extension of slavery but nevertheless he added that he hated the Kansas Act because, he said, of the monstrous injustice of slavery and because it deprived the Republican example of its just influence in the world.[7]

In March 1857 the Supreme Court decided the significant case of *Dred Scott v. Sandford* in which a black man sued for his freedom on the ground that he had lived for years in a territory which was free. Chief Justice, Roger B Taney, took the opportunity to declare that black people were not citizens and were given no rights by the Constitution. Nor had Congress the right, he said, to bar slavery from any territory. Accordingly, Dred Scott, a slave, had no constitutional right to sue in a Federal Court. Lincoln denounced the decision arguing that,

> The authors of the Declaration of Independence never intended to say all were equal in color, size, intellect, moral developments or social capacity but they did consider all men created equal in certain inalienable rights among which are life, liberty and the pursuit of happiness.[8]

The New York *Tribune* called the decision a "wicked and false judgment".

When the supporters of the *Dred Scott* decision argued that the Founding Fathers had never intended that Congress should have the right to forbid slavery in any territory Lincoln responded that 21 of the 39 Founding Fathers, including Washington, had indeed legislated against slavery.

Formation of the Confederate States

On 18 May 1860 the Republican National Convention was held in Chicago where Lincoln was nominated as its candidate for President of the USA. In the election which followed Lincoln won every Northern state, with 1,866,463 popular votes in all, and was elected 16th President. Immediately after the election, the legislature of South Carolina called a convention

---

7. Roy P Basler (ed.) (1946), *Abraham Lincoln: His Speeches and Writings*, New York: Da Capo Press, p. 255.
8. Harry V Jaffa (2000), *A New Birth of Freedom: Abraham Lincoln and the Coming of the Civil War*, Lanham, MD: Rowman and Littlefield, pp. 299-300.

which voted unanimously for secession from the federal union. Within six weeks South Carolina had been joined by other Southern states, namely, Mississippi, Florida, Alabama, Georgia, Louisiana and Texas. In February 1861, a month before Lincoln took office, they formed themselves into the Confederate States of America with Jefferson Davis as provisional President. Virginia, North Carolina, Arkansas and Tennessee joined them later, after the Civil War had begun.

At his inaugural address on 4 March, Lincoln declared that the Union was perpetual, arguing that secession was futile and he stated his determination that the laws would be faithfully carried out in all states. Five weeks later the Confederates began the Civil War by attacking Fort Sumpter in Charleston harbour. Lincoln called a special session of Congress, summoned 75,000 militia, ordered the enlistment of 65,000 regulars and proclaimed a blockade of the southern ports. The Confederates enlisted 100,000 men. Lincoln responded by declaring:

> My paramount object in this struggle is to save the Union and it is not either to save or to destroy slavery. If I could save the Union without freeing any slaves, I would do it; and if I could save it by freeing all the slaves I would do it; and if I could save it by freeing some slaves and leaving others alone I would do that. What I do about slavery and the colored race I do because I believe it helps to save the Union.[9]

A large proportion of the people living in the North were opposed to holding the Union together by force. One group wished to let the South go in peace, and another wished to tempt her back into the Union by offering the hope of new slave territories and States. But Lincoln remained adamant in holding that the Federal Union had to be preserved.[10]

The Trent Affair

British recognition of the Confederacy and her entering war with the North were key hopes for the Confederates and such hopes were raised by the Trent Affair in November 1861. On the 8th of that month the USS *San Jacinto*,

---

9. Abraham Lincoln (1990), *Speeches and Writings*, New York: Da Capo Press, vol. ii. pp. 357-8.
10. Herbert Agar (1965), *Abraham Lincoln*, London: Collins, p. 91.

commanded by Union Captain Charles Wilkes, intercepted the British mail packet *RMS Trent* and captured two Confederate diplomats, James Mason and John Slidell. Public opinion in Britain was outraged and the British Government demanded an apology and release of the prisoners. In the USA feeling ran high for war against Britain but Lincoln was determined to avoid war and released the prisoners as well as disavowing Captain Wilkes's action. No apology was made but Lincoln succeeded by his skilful diplomacy which was evident throughout the Civil War despite his most quarrelsome Cabinet.

Slavery Abolished

On 1 January 1863 Lincoln declared that all slaves in states or parts of states then in rebellion should be free. And, on 19 November of that year he made a short speech of 261 words at the dedication of the Soldiers' National Cemetery in Gettysburg, Pennsylvania. Although hardly acknowledged at the time "The Gettysburgh Address" has since reverberated around the world. Their task, he said, was to promote a new birth of freedom in America by "government of the people, by the people, for the people". He added that blacks should be treated as equals politically and under the law but in a democracy the southern whites had a right to participate in the democracy. Finally, on 6 December 1865, Lincoln persuaded Congress to pass the 13th Amendment to the Constitution which officially abolished slavery and "involuntary service" (except for crimes, after conviction by due process) in the USA.

General Ulysses Grant brought the Civil War to an end when he secured the surrender of General Robert E Lee on 8 April 1865 at Appomattox Court House. In this bitter and hard fought war some 260,000 men died in the Confederate armies and some 360,000 men in the Union armies. But the North had succeeded and then, at the Republican Convention in June 1864, Lincoln was unanimously nominated for a second term as President. In the November elections he received 2,216,000 popular votes against his opponent's 1,800,000 and 212 electoral college votes against 21.

Assassination

On Good Friday 14 April 1865 at Ford's Theatre in Washington, Lincoln was shot by John Wilkes Booth,[11] a half-mad actor. He died the next morning. Today, he is remembered as one of the greatest USA Presidents and for his world-famous Gettysburg Address (above) . But the problems he had foreseen arising from the end of slavery and the harsh implementation of the demands of southern whites was, in his absence, to lead to disastrous consequences. In the words of one writer, had Lincoln not been assassinated,

> the South would have been saved 25 years of revengeful exploitation, the North 25 years of shame—and the [black people] might have been saved a large part of the mistreatment which still pursues them.[12]

---

11. Wilkes Booth escaped to Virginia where he was traced and shot dead by Union soldiers.
12. Herbert Agar, *Abraham Lincoln, Op. cit.* p. 135.

Chapter 13

Edward Coke
Champion of the Common Law

Sir Edward Coke, was born in Norfolk on 1 February 1552. He attended school in Norwich and went on to Trinity College, Cambridge before residing in Clifford's Inn, London and passing to the Inner Temple where he was called to the Bar in 1578. He became Solicitor-General in 1592 and speaker of the House of Commons the following year. Subsequently he had an outstanding influence on English law and politics during the 16th and 17th-centuries. He was a skilful lawyer, a great judge, an outstanding jurist and a remarkable parliamentary leader. He suffered imprisonment and risked his life in defence of freedom and of its essential ingredients, the principle of public trial, *habeas corpus*, the right to bail and that against self-incrimination.

Attorney-General
At first, however, his influence was not always exercised beneficially. He had a darker side and he is revealed at his worst when he was Attorney-General. In this role, in a series of notable state trials for treason he paid scant regard to both the law and evidence during his prosecution of the Earls of Essex and Southampton in 1600, Sir Walter Raleigh in 1603 and Guy Fawkes and the gunpowder plotters in 1605. Sometimes, as with Raleigh, he attacked the prisoner, who could not at that time be represented by counsel, with the full violence of his temper and ill-will. He exhibited rancour and brutality that would be not be permissible today.

A few samples from the prosecution of Raleigh for treason held in the Great Hall of Winchester Castle will give a flavour of the latitude permitted to counsel at the time.[1]

> *Coke to Raleigh*: Thou art a Monster; thou has an English face, but a Spanish heart. You incited Lord Cobham to raise money for rebellion on the Kingdom.
>
> *Raleigh*: Let me answer for myself. Your words cannot condemn me; my innocency is my defence. Prove one of those things, wherewith you have charged me and I will confess the whole of the Indictment.
>
> *Coke*: Thou shalt not.
>
> *Raleigh*: It concerns my life.
>
> *Coke*: I will track you out before I am done.
>
> *Raleigh*: I will wash my hand of the Indictment and die a true man to the King.
>
> *Coke*: You are the absolutest traitor that ever was.
>
> *Raleigh*: Your phrase will not prove it, Mr Attorney.
>
> *Coke*: (Pointing his finger at the prisoner) All that Cobham did was by thy instigation, thou viper; for I *thou* thee, thou traytor.
>
> *Raleigh*: It becometh not a man of quality and virtue to call me so; but I take comfort in it, it is all you can do.

Despite such browbeating Coke was unable to get the better of Raleigh. However, under torture Cobham had signed a "confession" of treason implicating Raleigh although he later withdrew it and wrote to Raleigh expressing remorse for having falsely accused him. Notwithstanding, Raleigh was found guilty and imprisoned in the Tower of London for 14 years. Ironically, this inveterate enemy of Spain was then executed for allegedly being a Spanish spy.

Restoring the Common Law

In spite of his early excesses, Coke turned and was another who was not only famous but also became a great lawyer. In 1606 he was appointed Chief Justice of the Court of Common Pleas. He subsequently gave great service to his country and the law in resisting extravagant claims for the royal prerogative. By his time the Common Law had sunk into such a melancholy

---

1. *A Compleat Collection of State Tryals for High Treason* (1719), 4 vols, p. 174.

state that it had led to a rise in the power of the Star Chamber and the Court of Chancery. Yet Coke believed the Common Law was well-nigh perfect, thereby reflecting a deep-seated national sentiment. And he saw it as his duty to restore it by restating all its principal doctrines including that of Bracton's time that the King was subject to God and the law. This radical task he accomplished in his *Reports*[2] and his four books of *Institutes of the Law of England*,[3] the latter forming together the most important legal treatise since Bracton.[4]

He was, in truth, with his numerous innovations and adaptations breathing new life into the stagnating medieval Common Law and giving it the transfusion of new blood it needed if it was to survive into the modern world. But its many defects were often compounded by his partiality and his uncritical acceptance of the weaker parts of the *Mirror of Justice,* an anonymous tract of about 1290. However, his work formed an essential part of his struggle against conciliar "justice" and the defects were in part offset when rapid changes in society pushed Coke into a great deal of updating. At the same time the legislature was also busy bringing some laws into line with changed conditions since there could be no lengthy stagnation at a period of our history so rich in social and political turmoil.

Coke's third book of *Institutes,* published in 1644 after his death, dealt with the criminal law and pleas of the Crown. It was written in English, he said in its Preface, because it so closely concerned all the subjects of the realm. Furthermore, he continued:

> Where some doth object against the laws of England that they are darke and hard to be understood, we have specially in these and other parts of the Institutes opened such windows, and made them so lightsome and easier to be understood, as he that hath but the light of nature (which Solomon called the candle of Almighty God—Prov. 20:27) adding industrie and diligence thereunto, may easily discerne the same.

2. Sir Edward Coke (1600-1642), *Reports,* Dublin: J. Moore.
3. Sir Edward Coke (1823), *1 Institute—Littleton,* 2 vols. (with notes by Francis Hargrave, Charles Butler, Hale (LCJ) and Nottingham (LCJ), *2-4 Institutes.* (1797), London: E. & R. Brooke.
4. Henry de Bracton, *De Legibus Et Consuetedinibus* (Of the Laws and Customs of England), Lib.Iii. F. 118. C, 1250.

The *Institutes* show that the criminal law of the time comprised the Common Law offences enumerated by Bracton as well as about 30 statutory felonies and as many misdemeanours. Still, in fact, a very small corpus of law by later standards, but developing fast and already a law of crimes compared with the days of Henry III when the criminal law consisted of only eleven known offences, almost all of which were capital.

Supremacy of the Common Law
Whereas James I saw the judges as civil servants whom he could ignore if he wished, Coke saw them as independent and unfettered except by the Common Law whose supremacy it was their duty to uphold. Accordingly, he stood up against the King and this was exemplified in *Glover v. Bishop of Coventry and Lichfield* (the *Commendam Case*).[5] The King sent a message to the judges telling them that they must not proceed with the case until he had been consulted.

Coke refused, saying, "Obedience to His Majesty's command to stay proceedings would have been a delay of justice, contrary to the law, and contrary to the oaths of the judges". The question was put to all the judges who, save for Coke, all agreed the proceedings should be stayed. In contrast, Coke declared that, "When this happens, I will do that which it shall be fit for a judge to do". One consequence was that Coke, the Chief Justice of the Court of Common Pleas, was transferred by James to be Chief Justice of the more limited Court of King's Bench in order to diminish the impact of his independence. In his three years at the head of the King's Bench, however, Coke constantly quarrelled with James and in 1616 he was suspended from the Privy Council and forbidden to go on circuit. Later in the same year he was dismissed.

Before that and considering the Common Law courts to be the legitimate courts of the land he had attacked the procedures of both the ecclesiastical High Commission and the Star Chamber. He ruled that the *ex officio* oath by which prisoners were forced to incriminate themselves was illegal. He constantly issued writs of *prohibition* to prevent these prerogative courts from hearing cases which would result in imprisonment for adultery and other

---

5. (1617) Hobart, p. 140.

civil offences. Using the writ of *habeas corpus* he also secured the release from prison of persons incarcerated by the ecclesiastical courts or committed for contempt by the Lord Chancellor. In other words, with these actions he was undermining the prerogative and also proclaiming the subordination of the Church and ecclesiastical law to the Common Law.

Fuller's Case

In 1607 an attempt was made by Puritans to have the Common Law judges declare the High Commission itself illegal. A Puritan MP and barrister named Nicholas Fuller was chosen as the weapon.[6] Two men who refused to take the *ex officio* oath had been jailed for contempt of court. Acting as counsel for them, Fuller boldly denied that the High Commission had any right to fine or imprison any subject and he obtained writs of *habeas corpus* for their temporary release until he could argue before the King's Bench that his clients were detained illegally.

However, before the King's Bench judges could meet, Archbishop Bancroft and other commissioners arraigned Fuller before them alleging scandalous statements, schism and malicious impeachment of the King's authority in ecclesiastical causes. Despite obtaining from the King's Bench a prohibition against a premature hearing, Fuller was convicted by the Commissioners, fined £200 and imprisoned in the Fleet Gaol. However, Coke's opinion that the Commission's jurisdiction was limited to extremely serious ecclesiastical cases only was accepted by the judges and the number of prohibitions that now flowed from the Common Law courts sent the high commissioners reeling. And, since in this instance the judges were unable to rely upon precedents they deemed the question to be one of constitutional law.

Refusal to Sit Down

Sensing the threat to his power from Coke, in the Autumn of 1611 the King issued a new High Commission in the Great Chamber of Lambeth Palace at which Coke and six other judges were included in an attempt to silence them. According to Coke's *Reports*[7] the Commission was solemnly read and "contained divers points against the laws and statutes of England; and when

---

6. *Fuller's Case*, 12 *Reports*, p. 41.
7. Sir Edward Coke, 12 *Reports*, pp. 88-89.

this was read all the judges rejoiced that they did not sit by force of it". Coke, however, blankly refused to accept its legality and declined to take the Oaths of Supremacy and Allegiance required of the commissioners.

As he continued,

> ... and all the time that the long commission was in reading, the oath in taking, and the oration made, I stood, and would not sit as I was requested by the archbishop and the lords; and so by my example did all the rest of the justices.

But, when later Coke was removed from the Court of Common Pleas the High Commission renewed its prerogative role. However, Coke's efforts were finally rewarded when it was swept away by the Long Parliament in July 1641.

When James argued that the law was founded upon reason and that he could claim reason as well as the judges Coke replied that:

> Whilst God has endowed your Majesty with excellent science as well as great gifts of nature, you are not learned in the laws of this your realm of England. That legal causes which concern the life or inheritance, or goods or fortunes, of your subjects are not to be decided by natural reason but by the artificial reason and judgment of law, which law is an art which requires long study and experience before a man can attain to the recognisance of it.[8]

Before finally giving way, James in an act of bravado, tried his hand at hearing a case in person but became so confused that he gave up in despair. "I could get on very well hearing one side only," he said, "but when both sides have been heard, by my soul I know not which is right".[9]

Prosecution of Peacham

In 1615 Edmund Peacham, a church rector, was charged with high treason for preparing rough notes for a sermon which was never preached or published or intended to be. Peacham had predicted that James would meet a violent death. The King was so upset by this that every night he barricaded

---

8. *Ibid*, pp. 63b-65.
9. Lord John Campbell (1849), *Lives of the Chief Justices of England*, London: John Murray, vol. i. pp. 272-3.

his room with feather beds. However, the rector did also justify rebellion against oppression. To circumvent his Chief Justice, King James sought the opinions of the judges individually. Coke, in response, contended that the judges should not be approached at all, even as a body, on any criminal case that might come before them judicially.[10]

Since not only Coke but also some of his brother judges could not accept that Peacham was guilty of treason, James, who was utterly determined to ensure his conviction, put the case in the hands of Coke's adversaries, Chief Baron Tenfold and Serjeant Montague, a brother of the Bishop of Bath and Wells who claimed Peacham had libelled him. Not surprisingly they had no difficulty in finding Peacham guilty, although, for some reason, he was not executed. He had, however, been tortured on the rack before, during and after his examination prior to the trial and died of disease in Taunton Gaol after this. Public opinion was outraged and supported Coke.

Parliamentary Opposition

At the end of 1620, with all hope of returning to the judiciary gone, Coke again became an MP, joined the parliamentary opposition and soon became its leader. James was again in conflict with the House of Commons, this time over his desire to marry his son to the Infanta Maria of Spain in order to form an alliance with that country.

Coke began to work with powerful parliamentary figures such as the eloquent Sir Robert Phelips, Sir Thomas Wentworth, John Pym and, from 1624, Sir John Eliot. This was in line with his belief that the supremacy of law was a powerful weapon in Parliament's opposition to the Stuarts' continued attempts to establish arbitrary rule. In the Parliament of 1621 he had proposed the setting up of a sub-committee for the establishment of freedom of speech for MPs and to firmly demonstrate the liberties and privileges of the House of Commons. This was followed by a 'Remonstrance for Liberty' which he drafted. But this was rejected by James who had Coke imprisoned in the Tower of London where he was held for eight months. It is said that on reaching his place of close confinement which had once been a kitchen

---

10. Sir Edward Coke, 3 *Institutes*. p. 29.

he found written on the door, "This room has long wanted a Cook"—which is how Coke's name was commonly pronounced.

The Petition of Right

By the time of the 1627 Parliament, martial law had been introduced and the country was in a state of siege. Arguing that *Magna Carta* was a fundamental law that could not be annulled by statute, Coke, at 77-years-of-age, drafted the Petition of Right[11] which confirmed the supremacy of the Common Law as the safeguard of the rights of the citizen. The king, however, sent a message to the Commons forbidding them to meddle with affairs of state. This breach of the Commons' privilege of free speech produced what has been called a "spectacle of passions" in the House. One MP went to the root of the matter saying, "We must speak now or forever hold our peace". This was a supreme moment in the struggle for freedom of speech in Parliament.

The Petition of Right also had a powerful influence across the Atlantic Ocean where its principles were adopted by the American Founding Fathers, particularly Thomas Jefferson. This petition, along with Coke's legal texts, formed the basis for the modern Common Law and the precedence of individual liberty over arbitrary government. They were written in the white heat of battle in defence of the Rule of Law under pressure from royal absolutism. Such was his influence that, even in his retirement, when it became known that Coke was about to publish a book Charles I moved to prevent it seeing the light of day.

The Petition of Right marked the summit of Coke's career. A few years afterwards, when he was over 80-years-old, he suffered a serious accident when his horse fell upon him whilst he was out riding and after that he was confined to the house. Not being an amiable man he had few close friends but he was able to enjoy the company of his earlier estranged and still attractive daughter, Frances, who came to take care of him. She was, in fact, still a refugee from the High Commission and when she returned to London after Coke's death she was placed in the forbidding Gate-House Prison near Westminster Abbey. However, she soon escaped disguised as a page boy.

---

11. (1628). 3 Charles I. c. 1.

Death

Coke's injuries from the accident probably contributed to his death at his home in Stoke Poges, near Windsor, on 3 September 1634. He was buried at his own request in the family vault in St. Mary's Parish Church at Tittleshall in his native Norfolk where a marble monument was erected in his memory with his effigy lying full length upon it, in judge's robes with ruff and coif. Eight shields hold armorial bearings.

As we have seen, Coke had his darker side and was revealed at his worst when, as Attorney-General, he prosecuted Sir Walter Raleigh and others for treason with scant regard to both the law and evidence. He also treated his wife, Lady Hatton, very badly and eventually left her and cut off her allowance of £2,000 a year. However, he is best remembered for his use of the Common Law against the prerogative courts. After all, the King did not dismiss him as Chief Justice of both the King's Bench and the Common Pleas without cause. He suffered imprisonment and risked his life in defence of freedom and of its essential ingredients, the principle of public trial, *habeas corpus,* the right to bail and against self-incrimination.

Once he was dead the King ordered that his study be sealed up. But he was remembered in Parliament, which ordered that his books be published, and the victory of the Rule of Law over arbitrary power, which he did so much to secure, is a lasting memorial to him and a triumph for civilisation.

Chapter 14

Thomas Jefferson
Visionary and Founding Father

Along with John Adams (see *Chapter 7*) and others, Thomas Jefferson was a Founding Father of the USA. Both he and Adams served the new nation. But whilst Adams was from farming stock and single-minded about his politics, Jefferson was a more urbane, sophisticated and diplomatic type of individual. Whereas Adams was out of his element when representing his country at the French court in Paris, Jefferson, like Benjamin Franklin, enjoyed the regal atmosphere and the flummery that flourished there. As a consequence, he favoured closer ties with France when Adams worked for a rapprochement with Great Britain with whom, on behalf of Congress, he led the negotiations for the eventual peace treaty. Their close friendship during the early struggle for independence inevitably frayed when later, as members of bitterly opposing parties, Adams became President with Jefferson as Vice-President, although they became reconciled later. Once they were too old for office they resumed their earlier friendship and entered into an extensive correspondence that pleased both of them.

Family and Youth

Jefferson, the leading author of the American Declaration of Independence, was born on 13 April 1743 at Shadwell, Virginia. His father, Peter, was a tobacco planter and surveyor who mapped the Northern Wilderness. His mother, Jan Randolph, was a member of one of Virginia's most prominent families of wealthy English and Scottish gentry. Thomas was the third of ten children, two of whom died in childhood. At 25 he married Martha Skelton and they were happily married until she died ten years later. During that time they had six children but, as often occurred at the time, only two of them reached adulthood.

In 1752, Jefferson started at a local school and at the age of nine was studying Latin, Greek and French. His elder sister Jane taught him to read and he learned to play the violin. After his father died in 1757, leaving him some 5,000 acres of land and dozens of slaves, he was taught the Classics, History and Science by James Maury. Eight years later, when he was 16, he entered the College of William and Mary in Williamsburg and studied Philosophy, Metaphysics and Mathematics. He toiled hard—it is said he frequently studied for 15 hours a day—and became proficient in languages, although, at this stage, he was not involved with legal studies. It was here he acquired his great love of wine. In 1762 he graduated with high honours.

Profession of Law
Although he had not studied law at college, and he still preferred science and the arts, at the age of 20 Jefferson made law his chosen profession in order, he said, to be of service to society. In accordance with usual practice he commenced an apprenticeship in a lawyer's office but soon struck out on a hard-working course of self-study. In all, he spent five years in reading law with William and Mary law professor and jurist George Wythe, who made him an Enlightenment figure. And, in 1767, at the age of 24 he was admitted to the Bar of the General Court in colonial Williamsburg with a determination to use the law in aid of an anti-British revolutionary Government. Nevertheless, he practised as counsel in hundreds of cases in the General Court which consisted of the colony's Governor and Council and had both original and appellate jurisdiction in criminal and civil cases. Jefferson also undertook cases in the inferior county courts for lower fees which were fixed by law. He seems to have been at ease in court with an appealing manner although he was not an outstanding orator. His work in the law did, however, lay the groundwork for his political life.

At the time in Virginia there were no law schools, few law books and no American law reports. Indeed, there was no clearly defined set of colonial laws. The law was the Common Law of England. As a consequence, he commenced a study of the works of Sir Edward Coke (see *Chapter 13*) which must have given him a good grounding in both the Common Law and constitutional law despite his calling Coke "an old dull scoundrel". He did, however, come in time to admire this champion of English rights and liberties who had a considerable effect upon all the American Founding Fathers.

In addition to his practice as a barrister, in 1769 Jefferson became the representative of the county of Albemarle in the Virginia House of Burgesses where he met George Washington and where he was in office until 1776. And, in 1774 he wrote a set of resolutions against the Coercive Acts passed at Westminster which were soon expanded into his first brilliant published treatise, *A Summary View of the Rights of British America.* In this he made the then novel suggestion that the colonists had the right to govern themselves and that the Westminster Parliament had no right to legislate for the colonies. Like Coke, he stressed both individual rights and liberty and the sovereignty of the nation. In doing so he gave a structure to the rising demand for independence in the American colonies. And the Rule of Law was at the core of all he wrote. For Jefferson, law was not only the essential cement for the fabric of society, it was truly ennobling.

He believed that the Rule of Law had its origins in Anglo-Saxon England, particularly with the laws of King Alfred the Great. The preamble to Alfred's book of laws had contained a translation of the Ten Commandments into English, numerous passages from the "Book of Exodus" and a brief account of apolistic history. Further, Alfred endeavoured to ensure that there was not to be one law for the rich and another for the poor.

Jefferson firmly considered that King Alfred's dooms, as they were known, formed the basis of Coke's works. He also agreed with Sir Matthew Hale (*Chapter 4*) and others that Christianity was part of the law of England despite this being difficult to prove. Jefferson used against the mother country the myth about Saxon law being the true law and argued that it was destroyed by the imposition of the "Norman Yoke" which commenced with the rule and laws of William the Conqueror and the Normans. It had taken the English Civil War to destroy the Norman Yoke and notwithstanding his earlier argument Jefferson at least welcomed with open arms the emerging Rule of Law that Britain then offered.

Virginia's Constitution

Soon after the outbreak of the American War of Independence, in June 1775, Jefferson was a delegate from Virginia to the Second Continental Congress. Whilst there he desired to return to Virginia to help write the state's Constitution. Instead, a year later he was appointed to a five-man committee to write the first draft of a declaration to accompany a resolution of the independence of the colonies following the dissolution of the union with Great Britain on 7 June 1776. Jefferson completed his draft using as a guide his own proposals for a Declaration of Rights for Virginia and other sources including John Adams. He wrote a stirring statement setting out the right of the colonists to rebel against the British Government and establish their own based upon the principle he made familiar that all men are created equal and have the inalienable rights to life, liberty and the pursuit of happiness. After some revisions were made by others it was presented to Congress and on 4 July 1776 the Declaration of Independence was approved.

It set out the idea of natural rights that would form the basis of constitutional government. But only in 1788 was the USA Constitution ratified as the basic law of that country. It promised a jury for all trials except impeachment, and later Amendments added the right to a speedy trial, the right for a defendant to obtain witnesses and face those accusing him and to have the assistance of counsel in his defence. This involved acceptance of the principles of the Common Law including adversary trial. Jefferson had played the dominant role in writing the Declaration and this was his finest hour.

In September 1776 he had managed to return to Virginia where he was elected to the House of Delegates. Here he set out to reform Virginia's system of law and within three years he had drafted 126 Bills. One of these was to rid the state of the death penalty for all crimes other than murder and treason but it was defeated.

From 1 June 1779 to 3 June 1781 he was the second Governor of Virginia having been preceded by Patrick Henry. He succeeded Benjamin Franklin as Minister to France in 1785 and four years later Washington appointed him Secretary of State. He was President of the USA from 4 March 1801 with Aaron Burr as Vice-President. In his two terms as President he secured the purchase of Louisiana from France and the prohibition of the slave trade.

And, he is the only president to have served two full terms without vetoing a single Bill of Congress.

Criminal Law Bill

When the American War of Independence had begun in the mid-1770s there were in Pennsylvania nearly 20 capital crimes but by 1794, largely as a result of Beccaria's (*Chapter 20*) influence, only murder in the first degree led to the gallows. Indeed, Jefferson read Beccaria's treatise in the original Italian and copied long passages into his commonplace book.[1] This also contained 26 extracts from Beccaria in Italian, all the long passages being cited in Jefferson's own handwriting.[2] However, even after the creation of the USA, in Jefferson's native Virginia, English criminal law still reigned with offenders variously hanged, whipped, pilloried, branded or dismembered. But Jefferson was opposed to capital punishment for all crimes except treason and wilful murder and, in 1785, he introduced into the Virginia legislature a clumsily worded but important *Bill for Proportioning Crimes and Punishments in Cases Heretofore Capital*, with Beccaria's *On Crimes and Punishments* mentioned in four footnotes.

He explained to Wythe,

> In style I have aimed at accuracy, brevity and simplicity ... Indeed, I wished to exhibit a sample of reformation in the barbarous style into which modern statutes have degenerated from their ancient simplicity.[3]

In some respects the Bill was flawed and it was eventually defeated by a single vote in December 1786. It was, however, later approved when submitted again in 1796. It is noteworthy that in the Bill Jefferson set out three cardinal principles which he derived from Beccaria. First, since punishment is an evil in itself, it is justified only so far as it produces greater happiness through the reformation of the criminal and the future prevention of crime.

---

1. Merrill D Peterson (1970), *Thomas Jefferson and The New Nation*, New York: Oxford University Press, p. 124.
2. Marcello Maestro (1973), *Cesare Beccaria and the Origins of Penal Reform*, Philadelphia: Temple University Press, p. 141.
3. Merrill D Peterson, *Thomas Jefferson and The New Nation*, Op. cit. p. 125.

Second, punishments more severe than necessary to prevent crimes defeat their object by "engaging the benevolence of mankind to withhold prosecutions, to smother testimony, or to listen to it with bias ...". Third, crimes are more effectively prevented by the certainty than by the severity of punishment. As a consequence, certain penalties should be clearly associated with certain crimes and justice should be swift and sure, protected from judicial caprice and special dispensations of any kind. As he remarked, "Let mercy be the character of the law-giver, but let the judge be a mere machine".[4]

Nevertheless, he was sometimes at cross-purposes with his own beliefs. In Virginia the practices of gouging out of eyes and the biting off of ears were endemic. One observer recorded,

> I have seen a fellow, reckoned a great adept in gouging who constantly kept the nails of both his thumbs and second fingers very long and pointed; nay, to prevent their breaking or splitting ... he hardened every evening in a candle.

Considering which punishments would be appropriate for such crimes as rape, sodomy, maiming and disfiguring, Jefferson wanted the punishment to be retaliation in kind, although his mind was repelled by the idea. And, 40 years later he was puzzled to account for the sanction given to this "revolting principle"[5] However, it was a "principle" that with modifications Jeremy Bentham was also to embrace.

Jefferson and the Rule of Law

Jefferson"s dedication to the Rule of Law is clear from his determination to secure an American *Bill of Rights*. As Alistair Cooke has written:

> There might have been no workable Constitution, and no all-powerful Court, if the Founding Fathers had not listened, though rather late in the day, to an American who was not present in Philadelphia. He is the missing giant of the Constitutional Convention, Thomas Jefferson. He was in Paris as Minister to France, and he heard with alarm that George Mason had failed to impress on the Convention the vital need for a written Bill of Rights. He unceasingly nagged

---

4. *Ibid.* p. 126.
5. *Ibid.* p. 127.

every influential man he knew until he got it. Looking around him in France, Jefferson was a daily witness to the old indignities and assaults on personal liberty that the Constitution had failed to prohibit. And he wrote home continually that it was not enough to presume the sanctity of those human rights whose violation was all too familiar to the Founding Fathers. You must, he wrote, "specify" those liberties and put them down on paper.[6]

Within four years, on 15 December 1791, ten Amendments of the Constitution were ratified as the *Bill of Rights.* Six of them are crucial ingredients of the Rule of Law. They are:

1. The right of the people to be secure in their persons, houses, papers, and effects, against unreasonable searches and seizures, shall not be violated, and no Warrants shall issue, but upon probable cause, supported by Oath or affirmation, and particularly describing the place to be searched, and the persons or things to be seized.
2. No person shall be held to answer for a capital, or otherwise infamous crime, unless on a presentment or indictment of a Grand Jury, except in cases arising in the land or naval forces, or in the Militia, when in actual service in time of War or public danger; nor shall any person be subject for the same offence to be twice put in jeopardy of life or limb; nor shall be compelled in any criminal case to be a witness against himself, nor be deprived of life, liberty, or property, without due process of law; nor shall private property be taken for public use, without just compensation.
3. In all criminal prosecutions, the accused shall enjoy the right to a speedy and public trial, by an impartial jury of the State and district wherein the crime shall have been committed, which district shall have been previously ascertained by law, and to be informed of the nature and cause of the accusation; to be confronted with the witnesses against him; to have compulsory process for obtaining witnesses in his favour, and to have the Assistance of Counsel for his defence.
4. In Suits at Common Law, where the value in controversy shall exceed twenty dollars, the right of trial by jury shall be preserved, and no fact

---

6. *Alistair Cooke's America* (1973), London: British Broadcasting Corporation, p. 147.

tried by a jury shall be otherwise re-examined in any Court of the USA, than according to the rules of the Common Law.
5. Excessive bail shall not be required, nor excessive fines imposed, nor cruel and unusual punishments inflicted.
6. The enumeration in the Constitution of certain rights shall not be construed to deny or disparage others retained by the people.

Trial by Jury

It is clear that by the right to trial by jury in the *Bill of Rights,* Jefferson intended to go beyond the position in England where the jury were never allowed to interpret the law — that was for the judge alone in all cases. Jefferson said in 1782, in his *Notes on the State of Virginia,*

> ... it is usual for the jurors to decide the fact, and to refer the law arising on it to the decision of the judges. But this division of the subject lies with their discretion only. And if the question relates to any point of public liberty, or if it be one of those in which the judges may be suspected of bias, the jury undertake to decide both law and fact.

And, recommending trial by jury to the French in 1789, Jefferson wrote to Tom Paine,

> I consider ... [trial by jury] as the only anchor yet imagined by man, by which a government can be held to their principles of its constitution.

He also supported the reform of other aspects of England's outdated court system.

Death

Jefferson and his wife Martha had five daughters, and one son who was stillborn. He died at the neoclassical mansion he had constructed known as Monticello, in Charlottesville, Virginia, surrounded by his family, on 4 July 1826. Appropriately it was the 50th anniversary of the ratification of the American Declaration of Independence. He died a few hours before John Adams his friend and political rival, both of whom had fought for independence for the American colonies. He is regarded by many as the greatest American who ever lived and the greatest President of the USA although his conflict with Adams resulted in divisions that were unhelpful to the progress of that country. But, in addition to all his great achievements as legislator, statesman and President, he is also remembered for his constant attachment to, and advocacy of, the Rule of Law.

Twenty Famous Lawyers

Chapter 15

Shami Chakrabati
Equality, Respect and Human Rights

Director of Liberty

Shami Chakrabarti was born on 16 June 1969 in the London Borough of Harrow. She was brought up by her Calcutta-born Hindu-Bengali parents and her father, Mintoo, a bookkeeper was a strong influence on her interest in civil liberties. Her mother was a shop assistant. Her early education was first at Bentley Wood High School, a girls' comprehensive in Stanmore, Middlesex, and then at Harrow Weald Sixth Form College where she achieved three A-levels. From there she went to the London School of Economics to read law and she graduated there with an LLB degree. She qualified as a barrister in 1994 and did a pupillage at 39 Essex Street Chambers before working from 1996 as a lawyer at the Home Office on, among other things, the implementation of the Human Rights Act 1998, asylum and criminal justice. These aspects of the law were dear to her but she was, however, not entirely in tune with officials who wanted to deal only with high profile issues. As a consequence, she claimed that Home Secretaries should be banned from making new laws for five years. Instead they should concentrate on actually achieving positive outputs other than by legislation.

Eventually she resigned and joined Liberty, formerly the National Council for Civil Liberties, as in-house counsel on 8 September 2001 — the day before the terrorist assault on the twin towers in New York. Her influence as Director of Liberty, which she became in 2003, has been enormous and she is the Chancellor of Oxford Brookes University.

Human Rights Cases

When at the age of 12 Shami Shakrabati said that the Yorkshire Ripper should be executed her father asked, if she was sent to the gallows after being wrongly convicted, how would she feel knowing she was not guilty? That caused something to spark in her, she said later, and this was reinforced by her admiration for the American lawyer, Atticus Finch, in the book *To Kill a Mockingbird* and made her determined to become a lawyer. Like Martin Luther King she believes that the arc of history bends towards justice. She is married to Martyn Hopper, a litigation partner in the City law firm of Herbert Smith and they live with their son in South London.

As Director of Liberty, Chakrabarti exercises an independent mind. In politics she has opposed anti-terror legislation, identity cards, extraordinary rendition and detention without charge for 42 days as being serious threats to civil liberties. She has spoken up for detainees at Guantánamo Bay, defended trial by jury, told Muslims that they could not outlaw jokes against Islam and attacked the indiscriminate use of anti-social behaviour orders (which were later replaced). On 16 January 2012 she was the lead signatory to a letter to *The Times* newspaper calling upon the government to increase the minimum age of criminal responsibility from ten to at least 12 years. The letter said that the age of ten makes society less safe and delivers counter-productive outcomes for children for whom early adolescence is a period of marked neurodevelopmental immaturity. Furthermore, their lack of competence to participate in criminal justice proceedings reduces the likelihood of determining the truth and achieving justice.

> Robust action, outside the youth justice system, to deal with child offenders aged ten and eleven would serve justice more effectively and better prevent future crime.

The Work of Liberty

Liberty is concerned among other things with human rights, it fights discrimination and torture and campaigns for free speech and protest, fair trials and victims' rights. To give a few examples of cases in which that organization has been involved:

R (W) v. Commissioner of Police for the Metropolis. (2005) EWCA Civ 458
On an application by Liberty in July 2005 it was held that section 30(6) Anti-Social Behaviour Act of 2003 did not confer on the police power to use *force* in removing a person to his or her place of residence. The power was permissive not coercive and if the person concerned was acting legally his or her consent was required.

Roche v. UK (2006) 42 EHRR 30
In the early 1960s a serviceman (Roche) took part in mustard gas tests at the Porton Down chemical weapons research centre. He was not made aware of the nature of the tests. When, later in life, he developed health problems he asked for information on what substances had been used in the tests but could get no satisfactory answer. Liberty took the case to the European Court of Human Rights which found that the attitude of the government breached Roche's human rights under Article 8 of the European Convention on Human Rights. Liberty then represented Roche successfully on his appeal against the refusal of a disablement pension.

R (Watkins-Singh) v. Aberdare Girls' High School (2008) EWHC 1865
In July 2008 Watkins-Singh was excluded from her school for wearing in school the *kara*—a Sikh bracelet. Liberty took her case to court which held that the case involved both race and religious discrimination. Girls of other races and religions were allowed to wear bracelets indicating their race or religion and the school was reminded that section 71 of the Race Relations Act 1976 provided that schools should end unlawful racial discrimination and promote good relations between persons of different racial groups.

R (AM) v. Home Department (2009) EWCA Civ 747
In November 2006 a major disturbance occurred at Harmondsworth Immigration Removal Centre. Some detainees were locked in their cells for long periods without food, water or toilet facilities. There were also allegations of assaults on detainees by staff. The Court of Appeal found the government in breach of Article 3 of the European Convention on Human Rights by refusing Liberty's request for an independent inquiry into allegations of inhuman and degrading treatment.

Paton v. Poole Borough Council (2010) (unreported)

In 2010 Jenny Paton and her family were subjected to surveillance by Poole Council in Dorset for three weeks in order to check whether they were living in the catchment area for the school they wanted their youngest child to go to or were faking their address. In order to do this the council used powers under the Regulation of Investigatory Powers Act of 2000. Liberty helped the family appeal to the Investigatory Powers Tribunal, a body which normally sits and considers cases in secret. Following an open public hearing the tribunal ruled that the Council had acted outside its powers under the Act and violated the family's rights under Article 8.

Conflict with a Minister

Chakrabarti is a frequent contributor to television and radio programmes and various newspapers on human rights and civil liberties issues. She was described by *The Times* as "the most effective public affairs lobbyist of the past 20 years". In 2006, she was shortlisted in the Channel 4 TV Political Awards for the "Most Inspiring Political Figure". When the public voted, she came second to Jamie Oliver (a TV chef) and gained more votes than David Cameron, Bob Geldorf and Tony Blair.[1] She is not only a governor of the London School of Economics and the British Film Institute but also a Master of the Bench of the Middle Temple and a Commander of the Order of the British Empire (CBE).

In June 2008 Shami Chakrabarti crossed swords with Andy Burnham MP, the then Secretary of State for Culture, Media and Sport. Conservative MP and Shadow Home Secretary, David Davis, had resigned that post in order to force a by-election over the proposed 42-day detention for terror suspects. Before doing so he consulted Chakrabarti and Nick Clegg, leader of the Liberal-Democrats. Burnham claimed that it was odd that a "man who was, and still is I believe, an exponent of capital punishment" was having "late-night, hand-wringing, heart-melting phone calls with Shami Chakrabarti". Chakrabarti immediately wrote to Burnham accusing him of "innuendo and attempted character assassination" and demanded a written apology. This she received.[2]

---

1. Channel Four Political Awards, 2007.
2. *Daily Telegraph*. 21 June 2008.

LSE and Saif al-Islam Gaddafi

She was on the governing board of the London School of Economics when it accepted a donation of one and a half million pounds from Saif al-Islam Gaddafi, son of the late-Libyan dictator, Muammar Gaddafi. But she was not at the meeting which accepted the donation and, indeed, complained to the board about the School's links with Libya.[3] The Director of LSE at the time, Howard Davies, resigned over the ensuing outcry citing "personal error of judgement" while insisting that the gift did not undermine LSE's independence. At the request of the LSE, Lord Woolf conducted an inquiry into the matter and his report on 30 November 2011 was accepted by the school and suggested reforms were carried out.

The Leveson Inquiry

In July 2011 it was announced that Chakrabarti had been appointed, without pay to herself or Liberty in whose employment she remained, to the panel of the Leveson Inquiry—a high profile judicial inquiry into phone-hacking in the United Kingdom. Appeal Court judge, Lord Justice Leveson, led the inquiry which sat for 12 months. She described her appointment as "a daunting privilege" and said that it reflected Liberty's "belief in an appropriate balance between personal privacy and media freedom and above all in the Rule of Law".

To John Gaunt, a columnist on *The Sun* newspaper she is the most dangerous woman in Britain.[4] Her danger was to the forces of corruption in the country and her impact on the British legal scene is best summed up by the comment of Rabinder Singh QC of Matrix Chambers:

> I have found her to be a lawyer of the utmost brilliance and integrity. Since moving to Liberty she has combined a real knowledge of legal issues with a passionate commitment to the campaigning side of her job.

---

3. http://www.liberty-human-rights.org.uk/news/2011/liberty-s-director-and-the-lse.php
4. Original *Sun* comment not available but see a report in *The Guardian* of 4 April 2008.

Chapter 16

James Fitzjames Stephen
Codes and Colonies

Prominent Victorian Figure

James Fitzjames Stephen was born in Kensington, West London on 3 March 1829. He became a prominent and powerful figure of the Victorian age and was often likened to Samuel Johnson for his physical presence and his robust style of controversy. His contribution to the rapidly changing social order of his day was profound, if contentious. He was at the centre of the controversies on science, religion, literature and morality of the times. But deep down he believed coercion was essential to establishing freedom and wrote in his book, *Liberty, Equality, Fraternity*,[1] that it was "only under the protection of a powerful, well-organized and intelligent Government that any liberty can exist at all". In this he was a 19th-century precursor of Thatcherism. Above all, he made a marked impression on criminal law, not only in England but on criminal law codes in India, Australia, New Zealand and Canada.

Stephen's grandfather was close to William Wilberforce in campaigning against the slave trade and his father, as Counsel for the Colonial Office, drew in a single weekend the 26-page Slavery Emancipation Act of 1831 that abolished the obscenity of black slavery two years later.[2] This background gave young Stephen a grounding in liberal ethics but his upbringing was rigid and austere and in some respects he dramatically moved away from the ideals of his father.

---

1. James Fitzjames Stephen (1873), *Liberty, Equality, Fraternity*, London: Smith, Elder & Co.
2. 3 & 4 Will. IV. c. 73.

Schools of Life

Stephen was called to the Bar by the Inner Temple on 26 January 1854 and then obtained an LLB degree at London University. He soon joined the Midland Circuit where he said he learned that the criminal courts and their "customers" mirrored the multi-faceted kaleidoscope of human life; what he called the sorrow and despair, the tragedy and generosity — even the happiness. He always believed that,

> A criminal court is one of the great schools of life. We have here laid bare the foibles, the weaknesses, and the crimes of our fellow-creatures. Much that would otherwise remain hidden, is there disclosed to the whole world.[3]

However, what he saw as the dark nature of many criminals led to his well-known advocacy of retribution in punishment.

The Bacon Murders

On 25 July 1857 Stephen appeared on a "dock brief" (i.e. he was asked by the judge to defend an accused for a fixed fee of one guinea) at Lincoln Assizes to represent the 38-year-old Thomas Bacon charged with the wilful murder of his mother. With such a high profile case it was, as he himself said, his opportunity to make his fortune if he did well.

Bacon had previously been tried for arson and acquitted. He had also been tried jointly with his wife in the Spring of 1857 on a charge of murdering their two infant children by cutting their throats. In that case it was proved that his wife had committed the murder whilst insane. Although Bacon was acquitted of that murder, facts about the death of his mother were revealed during the course of the trial. As a consequence he was then charged with having poisoned his mother some three years earlier.

Stephen argued in Bacon's defence that the poisoner might have been the mad wife but the jury found the prisoner guilty. Nevertheless, in passing sentence the judge told Bacon that he had had a fair trial and the "advantage of a powerful address from a most able advocate". However, the case did nothing to enhance Stephen's fortune.

---

3. *Law Magazine and Law Review* (1864-5), vol. 18, p. 139.

Law and Morality

In 1863 Stephen published *A General View of the Criminal Law of England*,[4] widely considered to be a significant contribution to the politics and morality of the principles of jurisprudence. Sir William Holdsworth called it "the most original of all books on the criminal law".[5] And, in 1895, the *Law Journal* praised it as "pre-eminently the most readable English law book of the century".[6] Nonetheless, contrary to the growing feeling among lawyers that morality should form no part of the criminal law, Stephen considered that its administration should be based on morality. But he also went further and believed that the criminal law prevented crime by the use of terror and provided "a legitimate satisfaction for the passions of revenge".[7]

On the other hand he entirely approved of the rules of evidence which had been introduced only as recently as the 18th-century whilst failing to discover how they had been brought into being by William Garrow[8] and other Old Bailey lawyers. He believed that although the rules were largely exclusionary they should not lightly be tampered with if evil was to be avoided. As for procedure generally he argued that poor prisoners should be assisted by giving the police power and a duty to seek out and bring to court at public expense witnesses who could assist the defence.

Indian Penal Law

In the early 19th-century vast areas of India were controlled by the East India Company with a mixture of Mohammedan law and some aspects of English criminal law. The governing council of the company consisted of three members until the Charter Act of 1833 added a fourth member who, it provided, should attend meetings concerned with the making of laws and regulations. The first such member was Thomas Babington Macaulay who

---

4. James Fitzjames Stephen (1863), *A General View of the Criminal Law of England*, London and Cambridge: Macmillan & Co.
5. Sir William Holdsworth (1965), *A History of English Law*, London: Methuen & Co. Ltd and Sweet & Maxwell. Vol. xv. p. 290.
6. *Law Journal* (1895), vol. xxx. p. 393.
7. Stephen, *A General View of the Criminal Law of England, Op. cit*, pp. 98-9.
8. For Garrow's role in securing the rules of criminal evidence see John Hostettler and Richard Braby (2010), *Sir William Garrow: His Life, Times and Fight for Justice*, Sherfield-on-Loddon: Waterside Press.

single-handedly wrote a criminal code for India that was enacted in 1860 and was generally considered to be a great success. Stephen was subsequently appointed Law Member of the council in July 1869. He was fascinated by the sub-continent, writing to his mother before setting out on his journey there that, "Legally, morally, politically, and religiously, it appears to me, on the whole, nearly the most curious thing in the world". He explained that he had "an almost missionary feeling about the country and the office".[9]

Stephen remained in India from 12 December 1869 to April 1872 but in that short time he made an enormous impact not only on the criminal law but on his own political thinking and future conduct. He had an intense admiration for Macaulay's penal code but thought it necessary to fill in what he saw as one or two gaps. First, in accordance with his strong views in favour of capital punishment, he introduced the death penalty for attempted murder. And he added a section to punish a person who caused death by negligence, which, he considered, amounted to manslaughter. Then he inserted a provision that made it a crime to publish any writing with intent to produce rebellion. For this he was accused of tampering with the liberty of the press but he countered that intent was the essential ingredient of the crime.

He then turned his attention to criminal procedure. Unlike the Penal Code, the Code of Criminal Procedure bore little relationship to anything in England. In India there were different types of police, judges, magistrates and courts and jury trial was rare. There was no right of silence and there were first-class, second-class and third-class magistrates all having different powers. Stephen, therefore, prepared the draft of a new code, based upon English practice, which quickly became law.

As he saw it the criminal law was part of a system that enabled a handful of foreigners to rule about 200 million people. He explained that "the Penal Code, the Code of Criminal Procedure, and the institutions which they regulate, are somewhat grim presents for one people to make to another, and are little calculated to excite affection; but they are eminently well calculated to protect peaceful men and to beat down wrongdoers, to exhort respect, and to enforce obedience".[10]

---

9. *Stephen Papers (Correspondence)*, University of Cambridge Library, Add. 7349.
10. James Fitzjames Stephen (1883), *A History of the Criminal Law of England*, London, Macmillan & Co, vol. iii, pp. 344-5.

Anxious that a complete system of such codes should cover the entire Indian Empire in order to strengthen Britain's rule, Stephen set out on an extensive scheme of consolidation and codification of other parts of the law. As Sir Courtenay Ilbert, who succeeded Stephen as Law Member, so expressively put it, Stephen attacked his Indian work with, "grim joy, with fierce delight. His strong will overbore all obstacles". Continuing, he said,

> He left the Legislative Council breathless and staggering, conscious that they had accomplished unprecedented labours, but not free from some misgivings as to the quality and durability of the work for which they were partially responsible. The misgivings were not wholly without foundation. Fitzjames Stephen was a Cyclopean builder. He hurled together high blocks of rough hewn law. It is undeniable that he left behind him some hasty work in the Indian Statute Book, some defective courses of masonry which his successors had to remove and replace.[11]

Return from India

It is difficult to overestimate Stephen's impact on the English political scene following his Indian experiences. For years he had used his pen in England to write numerous articles in popular journals and engage in controversy with most of the important people of the day. His name was everywhere. Disraeli was later to write to Lord Lytton in 1881, "It is a thousand pities that J F Stephen is a Judge; he might have done anything and everything as a leader of the future Conservative party".

Despite not fulfilling that role, which it is extremely doubtful that he could have done successfully, this energetic and complex personality made a deep impression on late 19th-century politics in England as well as on English criminal law. The influence of his writings in favour of autocratic rule upheld by the criminal law, led Sir Ernest Barker in an influential book to describe them as,

---

11. Sir Courtenay Ilbert (1894). "Sir James Stephen as a Legislator", 10 *Law Quarterly Review*, p. 224.

the finest exposition of conservative thought in the latter half of the 19th-century ... a frank and die-hard statement of the ideas dominant among the educated and governing classes of English society.[12]

Liberty, Equality, Fraternity

Whilst still in India Stephen had planned a book in reply to John Stuart Mill's *On Liberty* and when sailing up the Red Sea he found himself, "firing broadsides into John [Stuart] Mill for about three hours". Mill believed that government was a necessary evil whose influence and coercion should be restricted as far as possible. There should be substantial equality between all human beings in fraternity. Stephen rejected the whole idea and the articles written on his voyage home became his book *Liberty, Equality, Fraternity*, published in 1873.[13] It was the most complete exposition of his views on politics, the state, law, morality and religion and their interaction. Its essence is an emphasis on the absolute necessity and inevitability of coercion and force. He saw the law as a regulated force, with liberty dependent upon powerful government. There must be war, he said, or there would be evils worse than war. "Struggles there must and always will be, unless men stick like limpets or spin like weathercocks".[14] Wars determined the nature and liberty of nations and decided what should be men's religion, laws and morals. The only concession he made was that for the general good the use of force should be moderated, if possible by persuasion but reinforced by compulsion if necessary.

Criminal Code Bill

With the support of the Trades Union Congress Stephen used his experiences in India to produce a Draft Criminal Code for England. This also had the support of the Disraeli Conservative government but it ran into troubled waters in Parliament and, although later supported by a distinguished Royal Commission, it eventually sank without trace. Nevertheless, his influence led to the Criminal Code of Canada in 1892, a similar statute in New Zealand

---

12. Sir Ernest Barker (1928 edn.), *Political Thought in England, 1848-1914*, Oxford: Oxford University Press, p. 172.
13. James Fitzjames Stephen (1873), *Liberty, Equality, Fraternity*, London: Smith, Elder & Co.
14. *Ibid*, p. 96.

in 1883 and in Australia, three states, Queensland, Western Australia and Tasmania similarly codified their criminal law in 1901, 1902 and 1924 respectively. All these codes followed Stephen's code closely as their authors were happy to point out. He also had an impact on the Penal Codes of many of the Crown colonies of the time. The year 1883 also saw the publication of his influential *History of the Criminal Law of England* in three volumes.

Stephen as a Judge

Stephen was appointed as a judge of the High Court on 3 January 1879. One of the cases before him that excited the public mind was the trial of a 22-year-old Polish Jew named Israel Lipski. He was convicted at the Old Bailey in July 1887 of the brutal murder of a pregnant woman in Whitechapel, East London and was sentenced to death. The murdered woman, Miriam Angel, had endured nitric acid being poured down her throat whilst lying in bed after her husband had gone to work. The bedroom door was locked on the inside and Lipski, who was found unconscious under her bed with acid in his mouth, had purchased nitric acid earlier that morning. However, he claimed that he and the dead woman had both been attacked by two men to whom he had offered work.

At the end of the evidence Stephen began his summing-up to the jury by saying that he had "never known a case which presented so many remarkable and singular features". Although no motive had been established, and there was no evidence of sexual assault, he also found it necessary to add that if immorality were the motive it pointed to the act of one man rather than two. In fact, it was widely considered that the evidence had been insufficient to justify the verdict.

At this point a public appeal for support for Lipski was encouraged by the *Pall Mall Gazette*. Politically, its editor, Wickham Stead, was virulently hostile to the Home Secretary, H Matthews, and he denounced the judge as Mr "Injustice" Stephen. The appeal was addressed to the Home Secretary to commute the sentence on the ground that the evidence against the prisoner was weak. Stephen knew he would be consulted about a possible reprieve and by now he was himself beginning to experience some doubts. He had come to regret his remark to the jury about the immorality motive and confided to his wife that he did not exactly hit the right point in his summing-up. He was also concerned because the law would not allow an accused person to give evidence at his trial.

Accordingly, he requested a respite and this was granted. He then re-examined the whole case and carefully studied all the articles that had appeared in the newspapers. By now over 100 MPs had signed a request for a commutation of the sentence, and three of the jurors in the trial had sent in a petition to the same effect. In the House of Commons on Saturday 20 August the Home Secretary admitted in reply to a question that Stephen had indicated that there was something to be said in the prisoner's favour.[15] Curiously, shortly afterwards Stephen's hesitation evaporated and he said he could find no reason to doubt the verdict.

Prior to that, however, Lipski confessed to the murder saying that he had purchased the poison for suicide and had killed the victim in a panic during an attempted robbery. Yet many people still retained doubts particularly as suicide seemed doubtful when Lipski was just starting up a new business about which he was very happy. Nevertheless, a reprieve was denied and he was executed the following day. It had been "a most dreadful affair", wrote Stephen, adding, "I hardly ever remember so infamous and horrible a story."

The Trial of Mrs Maybrick
Despite that remark there can be no doubt that the most difficult case Stephen had to face as a judge was the trial of Florence Maybrick in 1889. It followed the death of her husband, James Maybrick, an energetic, ruthless cotton broker, at their home on 11 May that year in what were alleged by interested parties from his family to be mysterious circumstances. Their hatred of the widow was manifest. He had married his wife Florence in 1881, whilst on business in the USA, when he was 42 and she a lively 18-year-old American. At the time he was already in the habit of taking dangerous drugs daily as a tonic, including arsenic and strychnine. He continued to do so for the remainder of his life.

Shortly before Maybrick's death his wife purchased some fly-papers which contained arsenic which she, and many other women at that time, used for cosmetic purposes. She bought them locally and quite openly from people

---
15. *Hansard* (1887), vol. 319, col. 364.

who knew her. At the same time she gravely warned her husband's doctors of the ill-effects of the enormous quantity of drugs he was openly taking. Indeed, after his death 154 bottles of medicine made up by 29 different chemists were found by the police in his office desk and at his home. Enough, it was said, to kill the population of Liverpool.

Mrs Maybrick was, however, arrested and charged with his murder at Liverpool Assizes where Stephen was sitting. There were suggestions that the police were improperly building a case against her. Various important witnesses were not called at the trial. The local press was openly hostile. In view of the local prejudice against her the case should have been transferred to Manchester or the Old Bailey to ensure a fair jury trial but this was not done. Since public opinion was so inflamed against the widow it was disastrous that in his charge to the grand jury before the trial Stephen remarked that adultery might supply a strong motive "why she should wish to get rid of her husband". To make matters worse, after the date of the trial had been decided upon, a barrister applied to Stephen to fix a date for another trial which was to follow when Stephen said to him, "But Sir Charles Russell may very likely wish to plead guilty." Russell was the leading counsel for the defence of Mrs. Maybrick.

At the trial the medical evidence was to prove hopelessly conflicting. Maybrick's medical advisers had prescribed drugs with highly dangerous ingredients which only reinforced his own voluntary abuse of his system. Additionally, as there was only a minute amount of arsenic found in his body since he was in the care of a nurse prior to his death, it was never proved that he died of arsenic poisoning, let alone that his wife had poisoned him.

Consequently, during the trial which commenced on 31 July 1889 public opinion swung favourably towards the prisoner. When, on 7 August, she was found guilty and sentenced to death the judgment was greeted with astonishment. The local jury had taken only 38 minutes to reach their verdict and on the following day *The Times* newspaper concluded that,

> It is useless to disguise the fact that the public are not thoroughly convinced of the prisoner's guilt. It has been noticed by them that the doctors differed beyond all hope of agreement as to the cause of death.

Thoughts then turned to the summing-up of the judge. At the close of the evidence Stephen had addressed the jury for 12 and a half hours over two days yet, as we have seen, the jury deliberated for only 38 minutes. Stephen's summing-up was at first favourable to the accused but then, on the second day of his address to the jury, became violently hostile. Alexander MacDougall, a barrister of Lincoln's Inn, wrote a sustained and vitriolic attack on the judge arguing that his comments to the jury were not only partial against the accused but also "lacerated" her and encouraged the jury to find her guilty of murder because of her alleged adultery. "Murder by Motive" instead of "Murder by Arsenic" he called it.

Ignoring, or perhaps unaware, of Maybrick's own infidelities Stephen had indeed told the jury that, "it is easy enough to conceive how a horrible woman, in so terrible a position, might be assailed by some fearful and terrible temptation." MacDougall described this as "terrible language" intended to excite the jury and he asked, "Is it possible that any sane man could use it?"[16] Another writer[17] has also suggested that Stephen's mind was suffering from early attacks of the disease which two years later compelled him to retire from the Bench (see below). Furthermore, at the time of the trial, Stephen was writing to his friend Lord Lytton, "I do still now and then smoke an opium pipe as my nose requires one occasionally and is comforted by it." Of course, opium smoking was not then illegal.

An alternative view of the summing-up was given by the first Earl of Birkenhead (the renowned advocate and Lord Chancellor, F E Smith) in his book *Famous Trials*, where he wrote that he experienced no doubt that the summing-up was both fair and impartial.[18] This is not clear from reading it, however, and certainly it was not perceived so by the public at the time. As a result Stephen suffered a hostile reception from hissing and booing spectators when he left the court. Indeed, he had to be spirited away under a police guard. In contrast, Mrs Maybrick was cheered by the crowds as she was driven away in the prison van to Walton Gaol where she was later to hear the gallows being erected outside her cell.

---

16. Alexander MacDougall. (1891), *The Maybrick Case*, London: Bailliere, Tindal & Cox, p. 550.
17. H B Irving. (1927 edn.), *The Trial of Mrs. Maybrick*.
18. Earl of Birkenhead. (no date) *Famous Trials,*. London: Hutchinson & Co, p. 405.

Stephen slightly redeemed himself by ensuring that the sentence was subsequently reduced from death by hanging to penal servitude for life. However, the utterly astonishing reason given for this by the Home Secretary was that although Mrs Maybrick had administered the poison her husband may have died from other causes. At the trial it was not even proved that Mrs Maybrick had administered poison. Yet, in his summing-up to the jury Stephen had forcefully told them that, "It is *essential to this charge that the man died of poison,* and the poison suggested is arsenic" (Italics supplied). In fact, the medical evidence had shown that the small quantity of arsenic in the body was not sufficient to have produced death, apart from how it may have got there.

In the event Mrs Maybrick served 15 years imprisonment, suffering solitary confinement, hard labour and ill-health, before finally being released on 25 January 1904. In her book, *My Fifteen Lost Years,* she wrote,

> A time will come when the world will acknowledge that the verdict which was passed upon me is untenable. But what then? Who shall give me back the years I have spent within prison walls; the friends by whom I am forgotten; the children to whom I am dead, the sunshine; the winds of heaven; my woman's life. And all I have lost by this terrible injustice.[19]

With their minds poisoned against their mother by her husband's relatives who had gained financially from her sentence the children never were reconciled with her.

The strong feelings and the doubts the case aroused played some part in the subsequent setting up of the Court of Criminal Appeal. And, in his revised *General View of the Criminal Law of England,* Stephen wrote that as a judge he had dealt in all with 1,216 criminal cases and that Mrs Maybrick's was the only case in which there could be any doubt about the facts.[20] Clearly it worried him to the end, as well it might.

---

19. Florence Maybrick (1905), *My Fifteen Lost Years,* pp. 222-23.
20. James Fitzjames Stephen (1890), *A General View of the Criminal Law of England,* London: Macmillan & Co, p. 174.

Jack the Ripper

It has been suggested that James Maybrick was Jack the Ripper.[21] As we have seen, Maybrick dosed himself with arsenic and strychnine daily for the last 14 years of his life and this had traumatic effects upon his mind. Although he lived in Liverpool, Maybrick could have haunted London's East End as he had a brother in London whom he visited frequently. Furthermore, his business partner's London office which he attended regularly was within striking distance of where the Ripper's murders were carried out. And at some point officers from Scotland Yard visited Liverpool to interview someone they suspected of being the Ripper. But who that was and what occurred cannot now be established because the relevant papers were destroyed.

There has been published a "Diary of Jack the Ripper" said to have been written by Maybrick but several experts have claimed it is a forgery. There have been numerous theories as to the identity of the serial killer but not one of them, including this involving Maybrick, has ever proved to be conclusive.

Opium

There is no doubt that towards the end of his life Stephen's mental health was in question. In 1885, whilst on the Derby Assizes, he suffered a serious stroke which mildly affected his mind. Then on 17 March 1890 he experienced a second stroke during the Exeter Assizes. His mind had started to wander and, after taking medical advice he resigned from the Bench on 7 April 1891.

As we have seen, at the time of the trial of Mrs Maybrick, Stephen had written to his friend Lord Lytton, that now and then he had smoked an opium pipe as his nose required one occasionally and was comforted by it. Of course, opium smoking was not only then legal but quite common. However, was his use of the drug merely occasional as he suggested? When the House of Commons carried a Resolution to stop the cultivation of the poppy in India he was outraged.[22] It would, he claimed, reduce by 20 per cent the income of the whole of the Empire. It could be compared with the millions of pounds spent to abolish slavery in the West Indies. And, in statements that would have had his father and grandfather turning in their

---

21. Paul H. Feldman (1997), *Jack the Ripper: The Final Chapter*, London: Virgin Books.
22. James Fitzjames Stephen (1891), "The Opium Resolution", *The Nineteenth Century*, vol. xxix. p. 851.

graves, he gratuitously added that the demand on the British conscience over slavery might have been exaggerated, and the "man and brother" cry might have been raised "more loudly than it should have been". The Opium War of 1842 that had introduced opium into China he brushed aside as past history.

As if all that were not enough he then declared that any alleged injury from opium smoking was "enormously exaggerated". On the contrary, in moderation it was highly beneficial. Further, it was a "self-regarding vice", although in his past dispute with John Stuart Mill he had not been so tolerant of such vices. Perhaps using his own experience of opium smoking he went on to claim that Indian opium was the most valuable kind of the drug.

> It is as champagne is to *vin ordinaire*, so that the only effect of stopping the growth of it in China would be to prevent the Chinese from using the best kind.

It is sad to think that smoking opium very likely contributed to his own growing mental frailty.

Subsequently he was created a baronet in recognition of his services and achievements. And in his last years he was made an honorary Fellow of Trinity College, Cambridge for eminence in science and literature, and Doctor of Laws at Oxford and Edinburgh Universities. To these awards were added his appointment as a corresponding member of the *Institut de France* and an honorary member of the American Academy of Arts and Science. These really sum things up. Despite his failing mental abilities towards the end of his life, and the sorry consequences for Mrs Maybrick, his contributions to society throughout his earlier life were noteworthy

The End

At the age of 65, Stephen died of Bright's disease at Ipswich on 11 March 1894. He was buried at Kensal Green Cemetery alongside his parents and his four children who had predeceased him. He was a man who, by any standard, made a deep impact on politics and law in England and India in the Victorian age. Whether he endeared himself to the people of these lands is another matter. As the contrast between his advocacy of force and vengeance on the one hand, and his warm relationships with his family and friends, on the other, testify, the paradox is that undoubtedly he would have cared.

Unlike many of his contemporaries, Stephen was able to see change as a fundamental of human existence and striving. That was his strength in understanding, interpreting and often opposing the philosophies of some of the giants of his time as well as of the past. As he wrote:

> The present is a mere film melting as we look at it. Our knowledge of the past depends on memory, our knowledge of the future on anticipation, and both memory and anticipation are fallible. The firmest of all conclusions and judgments are dependent on facts which, for aught we know, may have been otherwise in the past, may be otherwise in the future, and may at this moment present a totally different appearance to other intelligent beings from that which they present to ourselves.[23]

Without doubt Stephen was, and to some extent still is, famous but his insistence on coercion by the state and retribution in the law together with other failings or flaws, particularly when he was a judge, mean he cannot be regarded as a consistently great lawyer.

---

23. James Fitzjames Stephen, *Liberty, Equality, Fraternity, Op. cit.* p. 345. For Stephen's interaction with some of the giants of his time, such as Gladstone, see John Hostettler (1995), *Politics and Law in the Life of Sir James Fitzjames Stephen,* Chichester: Barry Rose Law Publishers.

Chapter 17

Edward Marshall Hall
Forensic Skills and Spell-binding Eloquence

Sir Edward Marshall Hall was born in Brighton on 16 September 1858 and was educated at Rugby School, and St John's College Cambridge where he took a law degree. His father was a well-known physician from whom the young Edward learnt a great deal about poisons which served him well in his career. In 1882 he married Ethel Moon but the marriage was unhappy. After they were legally separated in 1889 Ethel became pregnant by a young officer and died as a result of an illegal abortion. As a consequence the lover, the abortionist and several others were indicted for her murder[1] and the abortionist was found guilty of manslaughter. The effect of the circumstances of the death on Marshall Hall was profound. Unreasonably he had a deep sense of guilt over Ethel's abortion and this made him passionate in his defence of women maltreated by men. He practised in any event in the late-Victorian and Edwardian period when counsel were noted for their eloquent and dramatic histrionics in court and Marshall Hall exceeded them all in this and in the public attention he attracted. In some respects he resembled William Howe (*Chapter 3*) but without the criminality. He was described by Norman Birkett KC (*Chapter 9*), who knew him well, as an "erratic genius".[2]

---

1. Angus McLaren (1995), *A Prescription for Murder: The Victorian Serial Killings of Dr Thomas Neill Cream,* Chicago: University of Chicago Press,. p. 79.
2. Lord Birkett (1961), *Six Great Advocates,* London: Penguin Books, p. 9.

The Trial of Marie Hermann

This murder case in 1894 first made Marshall Hall's name widely known and set him on the road to fame. Marie Hermann was once an Austrian governess and music teacher but by this time she had become a prostitute. She was charged with the murder of one of her clients. The evidence against her showed that one night there had been loud noises coming from her room and a man's voice shouting "murder" three times. The next day she left with a large trunk which was later found to contain the body of a man who had died after being struck many times with an iron bar. The defence was that the man, when drunk, had attacked her with an iron bar which she, although a small woman, had managed to seize from him and hit him with several times. She had not intended to kill him and had endeavoured to restore him with brandy.

At the Old Bailey, Marshall Hall made a dramatic reconstruction of the incident before the jury, acting the part of Marie Hermann grappling for the iron bar to depict what he said had actually taken place. Indeed, on another occasion he had claimed that barristers and actors were alike and that "out of the vivid, living dream of somebody else's life, I have to create an atmosphere; for that is advocacy". It was the type of reconstruction he was also to use in other trials. In this case, in his final speech to the jury with tears pouring down his face, he said,

> Gentlemen of the Jury, I beg you to cast aside all prejudice because of this woman's way of life. I beg you to remember that these women are what men made them; even this woman was once a beautiful and innocent child.

At this Marie Hermann herself broke down and wept uncontrollably as did some members of the jury.

Slowly and emotionally counsel now said to the jury, "Gentlemen, on this evidence I almost dare you to find a verdict of guilty". Pointing to her in the dock, he continued, "Look at her, Gentlemen of the Jury, look at her. God never gave her a chance. Won't you? Won't you?" Such was the effect of his plea that Marie Hermann was acquitted of murder (which carried the death penalty) and found guilty of manslaughter. For this she was sentenced to six years penal servitude.

The Seddon Poisoning Trial

In 1910 Frederick Seddon was a 40-year-old well-to-do insurance superintendent living with his wife, Margaret, and five children in a large house at 63 Tollington Park, North London. He was obsessed with making money and decided to let the second floor of the house. As a consequence Eliza Barrow, a 49-year-old eccentric spinster moved in with her ward Ernest Grant, aged ten, on 26 July. She had a passion for gold and apparently a distrust of banks. She owned £1,500 in India stock, the lease of a public house bringing in £120 a year, £216 in a savings bank and £400 in gold. Seddon managed to persuade her to sign over to him a controlling interest in it all in return for which he promised he would take care of her for the rest of her life, giving her a small annuity and allowing her to live in his home rent free.

On 1 September 1911, Miss Barrow was taken ill. Ten days later she signed a will appointing Seddon as her executor and trustee and on 14 September she died. Without seeing the body her doctor gave a certificate which said that her death was due to epidemic diarrhoea. Within a few days the Seddons were seen to be in possession of large amounts of cash. However, they refused to pay for a proper funeral and Miss Barrow was buried in a public grave. This incensed her relatives who had not even been informed of her death. They complained to the authorities and the body was exhumed on November 15. The subsequent post-mortem examination proved conclusively that she had died as a result of arsenic poisoning.[3]

Seddon, and his wife who had attended Miss Barrow during her illness, were charged with her murder. The Attorney-General, Sir Rufus Isaacs, led for the prosecution and Marshall Hall for the defence. However, there was no direct evidence to show where the arsenic had come from. But other poisoners had used fly-papers which contained enough arsenic to kill and it could be extracted easily by boiling or soaking them in water. Furthermore, in her evidence, Mrs Seddon admitted having bought arsenic fly-papers and used them in Miss Barrow's room. Also, according to a local chemist the Seddon's 16-year-old daughter, Maggie, had purchased fly-papers from him. Giving evidence, however, she denied this which led Marshall Hall to bitterly attack Chief Inspector Ward for having interviewed the girl and

---

3. Sir Travers Humphreys (1955), *A Book of Trials: Personal Recollections of An Eminent Judge of the High Court*, London: Pan Books Ltd., p. 67.

framed questions to confuse her. In fact, she probably lied in court to protect her parents. Marshall Hall resisted all claims that Miss Barrow had been poisoned and claimed that she died by taking medicine containing arsenic.

Defying the advice of his counsel, Seddon insisted on giving evidence and in the witness box cut a sorry figure and displayed his callousness towards the deceased. He even suggested that she had drunk the water from the dishes of fly-paper placed in her room to keep away the flies. Marshall Hall always maintained that Seddon would have been acquitted had he not insisted on going into the witness box. Not surprisingly, since he was the person who benefitted from the death he was found guilty but his wife, who was totally dominated and used by him, was acquitted. Immediately before sentence of death was due to be passed Seddon made the masonic distress sign to the judge, Sir Thomas Bucknill, who like Seddon was a committed mason, asking him to overturn the jury's verdict in the name of "The Great Architect of the Universe". In response the judge, although embarrassed, told him that their brotherhood did not encourage crime, but condemned it.

The "Brides-in-the-Bath" Trial[4]

George Joseph Smith was a commonplace crook who graduated to murder. He was born on 11 January 1872 at 92 Roman Road, Bethnal Green in East London. From the age of nine, when he was sent to a reformatory, he was rarely in work but managed to survive by theft and by using his apparent charm to exploit women. On 26 August 1910 in Weymouth, using the name Henry Williams, he married Bessie Munday. The will that he persuaded her to make would benefit him to the amount of £2,579. 13s. 7d, a very considerable sum in those days when the average wage for a working man was barely £150 a year. She was found dead in the bath on 13 July 1911 at 80 High Street, Herne Bay. Following the opinion of Dr Frank French at the inquest, the jury found she had died by drowning. Smith, who had profited so richly from her will gave her a pauper's funeral in a common grave.

In the years 1913 and 1914 Smith married two other women who were also found dead in their baths in other parts of the country. In each case Smith benefitted substantially from their deaths and in each case the coroner's juries

---

4. See Brian P. Block and John Hostettler (2002), *Famous Case: Nine Trials that Changed the Law*, Sherfield-on-Loddon: Waterside Press, chap. 2.

reached a verdict of accidental death. However, the attention of the Metropolitan Police was drawn to the similarity of the deaths after one of their families spotted coincidences in a report in the national press and Smith was arrested. After appearing at Bow Street Magistrates' Court he was sent for trial at the Old Bailey where he was brought up before Mr Justice Scrutton on 22 June 1915 charged with the murder of Bessie Munday. Lasting until July 1 it was the longest and most sensational murder trial since that of the poisoner William Palmer, 60 years before. At the end Smith was found guilty after the jury had retired for only 20 minutes. He then appealed against conviction on a point of law.

Appeal

At the appeal before Lord Chief Justice Reading, Mr Justice Darling and Mr Justice Lush in the Court of Appeal, Smith was represented by Marshall Hall. He told the court that in Smith's trial for the murder of Bessie Munday evidence had been given of the deaths of two other women, Alice Burnham and Margaret Lofty, whom Smith had married and who were found dead in their baths. The evidence was inadmissible, he said, because no *prima facie* case had been made out against his client. The law was that some physical act must first be proved against the prisoner before evidence could be given of other matters in order to prove the nature of his act. He quoted Lord Reading himself who only a year before had said,

> We think that the ground upon which such [similar fact] evidence is admissible is that it is relevant to the question of the real intent of the accused in doing the acts.[5]

The perfectly clear inference was that there had to be a *prima facie* case before evidence of similar facts could be considered as admissible. Marshall Hall then pointed out that the House of Lords in *Christie*[6] had held that, "evidence as to other occasions should not be admitted unless and until the defence of accident or mistake, or absence of intention to insult, is definitely put forward" because its prejudicial influence on the jury would far outweigh its evidential value. The Lord Chief Justice interrupted at this point to say

---

5. (1914) *Boyle and Merchant*. 3 KB 339.
6. (1914) AC 545.

that the House of Lords had decided in *Christie* that it had become customary for judges to say that the value of such evidence was small compared with the prejudice created, but that the evidence was admissible. Marshall Hall continued:

> If the evidence regarding the death of Munday had been given first, and the prisoner had given evidence suggesting that her death was accidental, the other evidence would have been admissible; the test is whether there is sufficient evidence of the crime for which the prisoner is being tried for the judge to leave to the jury.

In what was becoming more of a conversation than an address by counsel, Lord Reading asked, "Do you object to this as the test? Is there, as a matter of law, *prima facie* evidence that the prisoner has committed the act charged against him? Sometimes, although there is evidence in law, the judge thinks it unsafe to leave the case to the jury". Marshall Hall accepted the test but said that,

> Even assuming that *prima facie* evidence was given, this was not a case in which evidence of other matters was admissible; the burden was on the prosecution to prove the intent. If there had been no cross-examination, and the prisoner did not give evidence or address the jury, the evidence could not be given.

Marshall Hall summed up his case and suggested that even if evidence was admissible that the three women died in their baths while the appellant was in the house, the matter was carried out much further here and evidence of all the surrounding circumstances in each case was given. The only effect was to prejudice Smith very gravely, and that evidence ought to have been excluded by the judge. He then quoted the trial judge at length to show that he had misdirected the jury but Lord Reading claimed the direction to the jury was accurate.

The prosecution then claimed that there was clear *prima facie* evidence that Smith had caused Munday's death by drowning. This was accepted by the judges, the appeal failed and Smith was executed. Yet there was not a scrap of evidence of any physical act by Smith that caused Munday's death.

It is difficult not to believe that the judges were reshaping the law relating to similar fact evidence to achieve what they considered was a just result.

After the trial Cecil Whiteley, one of the prosecuting counsel admitted the difficulty faced by the Crown in having no evidence of any act by the prisoner or of his presence in the bathroom when Bessie Munday met her death. Without the evidence of the deaths of the other two women he believed there may have been reasonable doubt of Smith's guilt in the minds of the jury who might well have acquitted him. There was a great deal of merit in Marshall Hall submission and although there can be little doubt of Smith's guilt the question remains, was the law properly applied?

The Green Bicycle Murder

One of Marshall Hall's most notable cases was *R v. Light* which became known as the Green Bicycle Murder trial (briefly mentioned earlier, in *Chapter 9* on Norman Birkett). The case involved the death of a young woman named Bella Wright who was killed by a bullet wound to the head in Little Stretton, near Leicester, on 5 July 1919. Earlier that day she had been seen cycling with Ronald Light, a First World War veteran who had suffered shell shock. Light denied the murder and the trial was held at Leicester Assizes held in Leicester Castle. Norman Birkett KC described Marshall Hall's entry into the court:

> He brought with him a strange magnetic quality that made itself felt in every part of the court. The spectators stirred with excitement at the sight of the man whose name was at that time a household word, and a faint murmur ran from floor to gallery. Marshall came, of course, with all the prestige of the greatest criminal defender of the day, and every eye was fixed upon him. He was a very handsome man, with a noble head and a most expressive face, and F E Smith's comment is not to be bettered: "Nobody could have been as wonderful as Marshall Hall then looked". When he addressed the judge it was seen that to his great good looks and majestic bearing there had been added perhaps the greatest gift of all in the armoury of an advocate—a most beautiful speaking voice.[7]

---

7. Lord Birkett, *Six Great Advocates, Op. cit*, p. 12.

Evidence in court showed that Light had once possessed a revolver similar to the one used to fire the shot that killed Bella. He had also disposed of his green bicycle in a canal after filing off its identifying numbers and had thrown away a revolver holster and some ammunition that fitted the type of revolver used in the murder. Two girls, aged 12 and 14 respectively, testified that on the day of the killing Light had chased them as they rode their bicycles through the countryside. He also had a record of improper conduct with young girls.

Light had met Bella on the evening of the murder and had accompanied her to her uncle George Measure's cottage where the uncle told her that he did not like Light's looks. Notwithstanding her uncle's warning she rode away with Light and was found dead some 30 minutes later. Although circumstantial, the evidence was so overwhelming that Marshall Hall advised Light to admit everything except the killing. He then submitted that the fatal shot could have been an accidental shot from a distance. This was likely, he claimed, because a shot at close range would have done more damage to the victim's face.

He said the prosecution case depended on the murder being premeditated and claimed that Light did not know Bella and therefore there could have been no premeditation. On this theory, and because in the witness box Light had been a calm and well-spoken former army officer standing accused of the murder of a factory girl, the jury acquitted him. The facts that a witness had seen him throw the bicycle into the River Soar and that he had lost his commission in the army were ignored.

Eloquence

According to Birkett, the jury were swept off their feet by Marshall Hall's eloquence and he wrote that,

> When he came to his peroration and depicted the figure of justice holding the scales until the presumption of innocence was put there to turn the scale in favour of the prisoner, not only were the jury manifestly impressed, but they, and indeed the whole court, were under a kind of spell.[8]

---

8. *Ibid.* p. 13.

A legendary figure

After his death Marshall Hall became almost a legendary figure in the public mind. He was compared with the great forensic orator of Rome, Hortensius, whose fame survives after 2,000 years because of his splendid physical presence, the adulation of the public and his powers of eloquent and persuasive speech.[9]

But in time the glamour has faded. Advocates are now expected to forgo histrionics, verbal attacks on witnesses and playing tricks upon juries—such as causing a distraction at some key point in an opponent's address to the jury or the evidence of a prosecution witness. Marshall Hall was a famous lawyer but, because he practised these methods, not among the greats of the profession like Thomas Erskine and Sir Matthew Hale who used powerful eloquence and persuasion without resorting to such devices.

---

9. *Ibid.* p. 9.

Twenty Famous Lawyers

Chapter 18

Gareth Peirce
Public Works, Private Life

Few people would accept that lawyers are renowned for hiding their light under a bushel. One lawyer, however, who does just that is Gareth Peirce, at least as far as her personal life is concerned. Although a brilliant lawyer she is seen as a very private person, shunning the limelight even when successful in high profile cases.

A Private Person
Born Jean Webb in 1940, she later changed her first name to Gareth, although as far as is known she has never divulged to anyone why she did so. She was educated at Cheltenham Ladies' College, proceeding first to the University of Oxford and later to the London School of Economics. In the 1960s she worked for a time in the USA as a journalist and experienced at first-hand the campaign for civil rights of Martin Luther King which left a deep and lasting impression on her. In the USA she married "Bill" Peirce, a writer and photographer, and returned to Britain in 1970. She now lives in Kentish Town, North London with her husband and has two adult sons, Nicholas and Zachary.

Radical Solicitor
After taking a postgraduate law degree at the LSE she was admitted as a solicitor by the Law Society on 15 December 1978. At the time she had already worked for four years as a law trainee in the firm of Benedict Birnberg.

On Birnberg's retirement in 1999 she became the senior partner in what became Birnberg, Peirce and Partners. Despite her retiring nature she is undoubtedly famous for her role in high-profile cases, particularly involving miscarriages of justice and alleged terrorism. As a consequence Birnberg claimed, "She has transformed the criminal justice scene in this country almost single-handedly".[1]

Notting Hill

Gareth Peirce has been associated with a range of high profile issues and campaigns, including when representing residents of Notting Hill in their encounters with the police and authorities during the years of turbulence that for many years affected that now gentrified part of West-London. One of her clients was the late Frank Crichlow, proprietor of the Mangrove Restaurant in Notting Hill's All Saints Road, which was hub for community activities (and raided by the police on occasions searching for illegal drugs or other illicit items). Tony Moore, who served as Divisional Commander at Notting Hill Police Station in the early-1980s and remembers Peirce from his time at Caledonian Road Police Station offers the following insights about her:

> Throughout most, if not all of his time at the Mangrove, Crichlow was able to turn to solicitor Gareth Peirce, whom [Michael] Mansfield [QC] described as "unique [with] a deep sense of injustice". More importantly, perhaps, in terms of representing Crichlow, her preparation in defending anyone when she believed an injustice had occurred, was "immaculate and immense [with] each brief or set of instructions" reading "like a book". She entered each case, suggested Mansfield "with a quiet and deliberate persistence [that was] unnerving". Thus "every dimension of a case [was] explored" and she was "capable of unravelling the most complex situations". There is no doubt that a number of divisional commanders at Notting Hill, and, indeed, police officers elsewhere, under-estimated Gareth Peirce over the years.[2]

---

1. *The Independent* newspaper (4 August 2002).
2. Tony Moore (2013), *Policing Notting Hill: Fifty Years of Turbulence*, Sherfield-on-Loddon: Waterside Press. The integral quotes are from Mansfield, Michael (2009), *Memoirs of a Radical Lawyer*, London: Bloomsbury, pp. 275/276.

Post Office Murder

The case which launched Peirce's career, before she had even qualified as a solicitor, is known as the "Luton Post Office Murder Case". On 10 September 1969 a gang of four attacked a post office and in the course of the robbery the postmaster, Reginald Stevens, was shot dead. As the robbers fled an eyewitness took the registration number of the car belonging to one of the four men, Alfred Matthews. After a police hunt for him, Matthews surrendered himself and was charged with murder. At subsequent identity parades he pointed the finger at David Cooper, Michael McMahon and Patrick Murphy as those who were with him in the raid. In exchange for turning Queen's evidence against them all charges against him were dropped.

The remaining three were charged with murder, found guilty and sentenced to imprisonment for life with a minimum tariff of 20 years. In 1972, on appeal in the light of fresh alibi evidence for Murphy, his conviction was quashed but the Lord Chief Justice left the other convictions in being. Apparently, with curious logic, on the basis that Matthews was correct in thinking that Cooper and McMahon had driven with him to Luton but was mistaken in believing that Murphy had been with them.

Fabricated Evidence

Peirce initiated a number of subsequent appeals believing that Commander Kenneth Drury, the senior investigating officer and head of the Metropolitan police Flying Squad, had, in fact, set up the robbery with Matthews. When it all went face-up they fabricated evidence against innocent men. Indeed, in the following year Drury was sent to prison for eight years for corruption. Ludovic Kennedy wrote a book about the case entitled *Wicked Beyond Belief* and within a month the men were released from prison. However, Cooper and McMahon died in 1993 and 1999 respectively without their innocence having been established.

Peirce persisted with appeals, however, and in March 2001 the Criminal Cases Review Commission referred the case back to the Court of Appeal for a sixth appeal. Subsequently, on 31 July 2003 the Court of Appeal quashed the convictions but, of course, too late for the victims of the miscarriage of justice.

Nevertheless, the Police and Criminal Evidence Act 1984 (PACE), which provided that statements by accused persons to the police should be tape-recorded and with a defence solicitor present, proved to be a turning point in the protection of suspects as well as securing more effective prosecution of crime.

High-Profile Trials

In a career of nearly 40-years the passionate advocacy and great attention to detail of Peirce has brought spectacular results and made her a thorn in the side of the legal establishment. Perhaps her greatest success was with the appeal in the case of the "Guildford Four" (*Chapter 8*). The original trial in 1974 was reported around the world and made into a powerful film entitled "In the Name of the Father". In the film, which highlighted terrifying examples of police callousness and torture, Peirce was played by Emma Thompson who received an Oscar for the portrayal (which Peirce is reported as having said she disliked).

It was the 1970s that produced the maxim "Innocent until proved Irish". It should be remembered, however, that at the time, in a black decade for the police, juries were bombarded with false confessions obtained under police torture and threats, with evidence that had been tampered with alongside relevant information being withheld from the defence and its lawyers.

Another high-profile trial in which Peirce played a prominent part was that of the "Birmingham Six" (*Chapter 19*). She also represented the family of Jean Charles de Menezes, who was shot seven times by Metropolitan policemen at Stockwell Underground station on 22 July 2005 in mistake for a suicide bomber. For endangering the public, rather than the unlawful killing of an innocent bystander, the police were ordered at the Old Bailey to pay a fine of £175 with costs of £385.000. She also represented the families of the victims of the *Marchioness* river boat disaster in 1989 when a pleasure cruiser and a barge collided on the River Thames causing the deaths of 30 people.

She acted for Judith Ward who had been wrongfully convicted in 1974 of a number of IRA bombings as well as Moazzam Begg who was held in extra-judicial detention by the American government in Gantánamo Bay. "She specialises in representing pariahs of society", said Begg. "I know because I am one of them".

Muslim Terrorist Suspects

More recently Peirce has defended a number of Muslim terrorist suspects in the UK including some who had returned from detention in Guantánamo Bay. She claimed that the UK and USA "had not launched a war on terror but a war on human rights".[3]

Similarly, speaking of her Muslim clients she said,

> We have lost our way in this country. We have entered a new dark age of injustice and it is frightening that we are overwhelmed by it. I know I am representing innocent people; innocent people who know that a jury they face will inevitably be predisposed to find them guilty.[4]

When asked in another *Guardian* interview[5] whether some of her clients had trained at al-Qaida camps she replied:

> Those men were thinking of fighting for the Chechens or for the Taliban before the allies invaded Afghanistan. I've represented these men for a very long time, men who are stigmatised as a threat to national security when they're not. I know that they are intelligent, thoughtful men.

In her work as a solicitor in England Gareth Peirce has shone as an outstanding human rights lawyer whose battles against miscarriages of justice have changed criminal law history. As a very private person her fame rests not on unbridled media exposure, which could have come easily, but simply on her cases and her single-minded dedication to securing justice.

---

3. *The Guardian* (31 January 2009).
4. *The Guardian* (1 April 2004).
5. *The Guardian* (12 October 2010).

Chapter 19

Alfred Denning
People's Judge and an Unlikely Celebrity

A Legend in His Own Lifetime
In the 20th-century Alfred Lord Denning's fame rested not only in England but spread across the countries of the Commonwealth. Lord Bingham, the Lord Chief Justice, said he was

> the best known and best loved judge of this, or perhaps any, generation. He was a legend in his own lifetime.

He was, indeed, a celebrated judge who left his mark on the development of English law as well as through the medium of TV and radio as a result of which he became something of a household name as someone who had risen through the judicial ranks with great speed, been chosen to lead a highly sensitive enquiry going to the heart of government and who might be prepared to "challenge authority" or stand up for "the little man". But, for reasons which will become clear, it is doubtful whether it can be claimed that he was a great judge and the passage of time has not been kind to his reputation.

Widely known, even in later life, as "Tom", he was born to Charles Denning, a draper, and his wife Clara in Whitchurch, Hampshire on 23 January 1899. His early education was at Andover Grammar School. His parents were not wealthy but he gained a place at Magdalen College, Oxford University with a grant. He went on to obtain a law degree and after being admitted to Lincoln's Inn he was called to the Bar on 13 June 1923. With astonishing rapidity he became a judge of the High Court in 1944. Fewer than five years later he was made a Lord Justice of Appeal. During his spell in the House of Lords he felt that he was involved in too few cases and that this was not the best forum in which to exercise his creativity in the law. He, therefore, returned to the Court of Appeal as Master of the Rolls in 1962, a position he held for 20 years. He was to serve as a judge in all for 38 years.

The High Trees House Case
In this case Denning, as a junior judge in 1946, changed the law and made his mark on the legal profession. His judgment, in re-assessing the strict rules of law concerning "consideration" (that under which a contract connotes some exchange of value involving both sides) and estoppel (a rule by which a person is not allowed to deny something he has previously asserted and which has been acted upon to his disadvantage by another) was controversial but it has never been overruled. The full title of the case is, *Central London Property Trust Ltd v. High Trees House Limited*.[1]

Here, Denning used an equitable doctrine to ensure justice as he saw it in a common law case. He thus prevented a party to the cause from insisting upon his strict legal rights when it would have been unjust to allow him to enforce them having regard to dealings which had taken place between the parties. He explained the principle involved in the later case of *Combe v. Combe* in 1951:

> Where one party has, by his words or conduct, made to the other a promise or assurance which was intended to affect the legal relations between them and to be acted on accordingly, then, once the other party has taken him at his word and acted on it, the one who gave the promise or assurance cannot afterwards be allowed to revert to the previous legal relations as if no such promise or assurance had been made by him; but he must accept their legal relations subject to the qualification which he himself has so introduced, even though it is not supported in point of law by any consideration but only by his word.

---

1. 1 (1946) 1. KB 133.

This law-making by a judge caused a furore in the legal profession and it was, and remains, controversial. In his book *The Discipline of Law*,[2] Denning argued that in "High Trees" he had helped to narrow the gap between the extreme rules of archaic law such as "consideration" and estoppel and the social necessities of the 20th-century. As such the case was the first of many attempts made by Denning to bring justice as he saw it into the law.

Capital Punishment

As a High Court judge Lord Denning was not averse to people being sentenced to death saying that it did not worry him in the least. He was one of the Law Lords who decided a controversial criminal case, namely *DPP v. Smith*[3] (also known as the case of Gypsy Jim Smith) when he was held guilty of the murder of a police officer. The circumstances of the offence were such that it is not too strong to say that the decision of the Law Lords shocked, and brought high level and devastating criticism from, important elements in both academic legal circles and among practising lawyers. *The Criminal Law Review* commented that,

> This remarkable decision lays down a test for the law of murder which is staggering in its severity. The only *mens rea* which the prosecution need prove, it seems, is an intention to do "something to someone".[4]

Furthermore, Denning was later to remark on the utility of capital punishment years after it had been abolished.[5]

The Profumo Affair

John Profumo was the Secretary of State for War in the British Government. At a party in 1961 he was introduced to Christine Keeler, a call girl,

---

2. Lord Denning (1979), *The Discipline of Law*, London: Butterworths, p. 197.
3. (1961) AC. 290. HL.
4. *The Criminal Law Review.* (1960), p. 766.
5. Terence Morris and Louis Blom-Cooper. (2011) *Fine Lines and Distinctions: Murder, Manslaughter and the Unlawful Taking of Human Life,* Sherfield-on-Loddon: Waterside Press, p. 171. Although *DPP v Smith* was a capital case, the Home Secretary indicated ahead of the appeal to the House of Lords that if the conviction was upheld, Smith would nonetheless be reprieved. The law of murder could thus be decided free of the practical ramifications.

and began an affair with her. She was also in a relationship with Yevgeni Ivanov a naval attaché at the London Embassy of the Soviet Union. When the position became public knowledge, Profumo made a statement to the House of Commons denying any impropriety in his relationship with Keeler. However, later he had to admit that he had lied to the House of Commons and in consequence he resigned from the Government.

On 21 June 1963 Harold Macmillan, Prime Minister, asked Denning to lead an inquiry into the circumstances of Profumo's retirement. The inquiry took 49 days and Denning's final report, delivered on 26 September, was 70,000 words long (and sold 105,000 copies, 4,000 of them in the first hour). The report blamed Profumo for causing the scandal by associating with Keeler and for his false statement in the House of Commons. It made Denning famous and was described as the raciest and most readable "Blue Book" ever published. On the other hand, it was also criticised as being a "whitewash", although this was a claim which Denning rejected.

Other Landmark Cases

Denning invented the *Mareva Injunction* (now known as the "freezing injunction"). Until this case, which gave rise to the cause of action known by the name Mareva, it was possible for an organization against whom a claim had been made to engage in delaying tactics and remove all of its assets to another jurisdiction where they could not be reached. Denning's judgment reversed the common law and gave the claimant in such a case a lien over such assets. The justice of the decision was clear but the grounds for overturning a longstanding practice were flimsy. Nonetheless, Denning later called the case the greatest piece of law reform in his time.[6]

In 1952 he established in the Court of Appeal the "deserted wife's equity" by ruling that a deserted wife occupying the matrimonial home had a personal licence to stay there.[7] This decision provoked disapproval among the judiciary and parts of the public. It was overruled by the House of Lords in another case[8] where it was held that the deserted wife had no licence to stay.

---

6. For a more detailed consideration, see Brian P. Block and John Hostettler (2002), *Famous Cases: Nine Trials that Changed the Law*, Sherfield-on-Loddon: Waterside Press, pp. 92-97.
7. *Bendall v. McWhirter* (1952) 2 QB 466.
8. *National Provincial Bank Ltd. v. Ainsworth* (1965) AC 1175.

This led to the enactment of the Matrimonial Homes Act of 1967 which partially restored Denning's judgment. He also ruled that an unmarried partner who contributes to buying or improving the home in which they live might claim a share under the law of trusts.

Denning gave the leading judgment in an important case in 1964.[9] Mrs Letang, on holiday in Cornwall, decided to lie down and rest on grass outside a hotel. A man named Cooper drove into the hotel car park and, not seeing Letang, ran over her legs. More than three years later she brought a case against Cooper in tort (i.e. alleging a civil wrong) claiming damages for her injuries. The normal tort for personal injuries is that of negligence which is governed by a three year statute of limitations. But Letang claimed damages instead under the tort of trespass to the person where the limit was six years. On appeal to the Court of Appeal, Denning, Denning and Lord Justice Danckwerts held that the tort of trespass could only be used if the injury was inflicted intentionally; if it was unintentional, only negligence could be used. Lord Justice Diplock dissented.

Prejudices

Denning gave judgment in some 2,000 reported cases and in many of them he changed the law for the better. However, he had prejudices that sometimes came to the fore. We have seen that he favoured the retention of the death penalty. And one of his worst judgments involved a student teacher sent down for having sex with her boyfriend in her hall of residence at university. Denning strongly approved of the university's sentence, saying that a young woman who behaved in such a way would never have made a teacher.

Civil Liberties

During the course of World War II Ronald Rubinstein, a well-known London solicitor, wrote a book entitled *John Citizen and the Law*[10] which endeavoured to explain English law to the layman. It was published by Penguin Books in 1948 and was so successful that it was said at the time to have sold more books in England than any other apart from the Bible. After Rubinstein's death the publishers asked his son, Christopher to edit the book for future

---

9. *Letang v. Cooper* (1964) 2 All ER 292. 1QB 232.
10. Ronald Rubinstein (1948), *John Citizen and the Law*, West Drayton: Penguin Books.

editions. Chris Rubinstein, who at that time was a partner of mine in our law firm, accepted the commission and on the first edition edited by him[11] he asked Lord Denning to write a Foreward. Denning did so.

When the next edited version became due Chris decided it was appropriate to include a chapter on civil liberties.[12] He asked Lord Denning if this would change his approval of the book and Denning withdrew his Forword. It is intriguing to wonder why Denning decided he did not want to be associated with this addition to the book.

Retirement

In a trial arising out of the Bristol race riots in 1982 he Denning suggested that some ethnic people might not be suitable as jurors, and that black defendants had used peremptory challenges to pack the jury with "as many coloured people as possible".[13] Two black jurors threatened to sue him for libel and with the Society of Black Lawyers and with sections of the press calling upon him to retire as a judge he decided that it was time to do so. In the summer of 1990, he remarked in a taped interview that if the "Guildford Four" had been hanged, "They'd probably have hanged the right men. Just not proved against them, that's all".[14] This was a serious misunderstanding of the serious miscarriage of justice that had occurred in their trial[15] and Denning had once again put his foot in it.

Earlier, in 1988, he had expressed a similar opinion with regard to the "Birmingham Six". In 1975 they were sentenced to life imprisonment for allegedly having committed murder and conspiring to cause explosions in Birmingham. In 1980 Denning upheld an appeal by the West Midlands police against a civil action by the "Birmingham Six" over injuries they received while in police custody. He said that if these six men were not guilty it would mean that the police were guilty of perjury, violence and threats and that the confessions they had made were involuntary and not properly admitted in evidence. That he said was an "appalling vista".

---

11. Christopher R. Rubinstein (1958), *John Citizen and the Law*. 4th edition, Harmondsworth: Penguin Books.
12. *Ibid.* (1963, 5th edition, Harmondsworth: Penguin Books.
13. Lord Denning (1982), *What Next in the Law*, London: Butterworths, p. 68.
14. Iris Freeman (1993), *Lord Denning: A Life*, London: Hutchinson, p. 412.
15. See *ante*, p. 60.

Notwithstanding, on 14 March 1991 the Court of Appeal overturned the convictions precisely on the grounds that the police had both fabricated and suppressed evidence. Yet, in 1988 Denning had said, "Hanging ought to be retained for murder most foul. We shouldn't have all these campaigns to get the "Birmingham Six" released if they'd been hanged. They'd have been forgotten, and the whole community would be satisfied". He added that it is better that some innocent men remain in jail than that the integrity of the English judicial system be impugned. As a result of assertions of this kind, he was reported to have himself become a target of terrorists although he frequently went about without noticeable protection; on one occasion when unveiling a bust of himself at the Law Courts in Winchester taunting them to "come and get him".[16] Famous he undoubtedly was, but his prejudices and sometimes his judgement in later life serve to prevent him from being remembered as a truly great lawyer.

The End

Denning was the last judge in England not to have a mandatory retirement age but clearly it was not proper that he continue on the Bench and his retirement came not a day too early. In retirement he returned to Whitchurch and by 1989 his health was failing. He celebrated his 100th birthday there on 23 January 1999 and on 5 March he died in the Royal Hampshire County Hospital in Winchester. Tributes came from the Lord Chancellor, judges, lawyers and from the Prime Minster, Tony Blair. Former Prime Ministers, Baroness Thatcher and Lord Callaghan also paid homage to the man known to many as "The People's Judge".

---

16. Personal communication.

Chapter 20

Cesare Beccaria
Crusader Against Torture

Cesare Beccaria did more to inspire reform of the medieval criminal law that still disfigured the English criminal justice system in the 18th-century than any other lawyer. At the time the death penalty existed for all felonies (which meant most crimes) including many of a minor nature such as stealing a handkerchief. And this murder by the state meant slow and painful strangulation on the gallows. No one was safe from it. Not surprisingly it excited widespread fear and horror. In Europe and many other countries across the globe that embraced the inquisitorial system of criminal procedure the situation was even worse with torture widely practised including the wheel which involved tearing apart the victims limbs. Except in England the Rule of Law was disregarded in favour of judicial ferocity and cruelty. Beccaria was to change that in many countries and although his thesis was to take hold in England only slowly, his influence gradually brought about vast changes through the influence of Jeremy Bentham (*Chapter 10*), Samuel Romilly and Lord John Russell.

On Crimes and Punishments
Beccaria was born on 15 March 1738, the eldest son of an aristocratic family in Milan a city of 120,000 people in Lombardy. Although he never practised as a lawyer he was awarded a law degree by the University of Pavia in 1758. He was virtually unknown when, on 12 April 1764, at the age of 26 he published in Livorno his short book entitled *On Crimes and Punishments* (*Dei Delitti e delle Pene* in its original Italian). Yet only a year later his fame

stretched worldwide because of the sheer genius of this book and its impact. Why then is he so little known today? The answer lies in the phenomenal success the book had when first published which resulted in his achievements becoming part of the fabric of our lives. As a consequence we take freedom from cruel criminal laws for granted and give little heed to how such freedom came about.

Beccaria battled—against venomous and unprincipled opposition from the Roman Catholic Church and many lawyers—for a humane legal system. Penal law was barbaric and in England we still had what Sir Robert Peel called the "Bloody Code" with hanging by the neck the penalty for over 200 felonies, with many of them of a trivial nature. This was not always carried out, however, thanks to the humanity of juries and royal pardons. Yet the situation in Europe was far worse.

It was against this background that the young Italian Count produced his bombshell of a book which had a profound influence on Bentham and Romilly in England, on Maria Theresa in Austria and Catherine the Great of Russia. Its influence even spread, as we have seen, to the Bill of Rights of the newly-independent American Republic through the insistence of Presidents John Adams (*Chapter 7*) and Thomas Jefferson (*Chapter 14*). In Europe it was immediately hailed by the leaders of the Enlightenment including Voltaire. It spread like wildfire with Maria Theresa and the Grand Duke Leopold of Tuscany publicly changing their laws in conformity with the principles of the book, whilst Catherine the Great asked Beccaria to go to Russia to oversee the implementation of his proposals that she was adopting. Sweden and Portugal also enacted new codes of criminal law based upon Beccaria's principles.

What Beccaria proposed was that torture and the death penalty, which together formed the binding cement of the European inquisitorial system in criminal law, should be abolished; that criminal trials should be prompt; and that punishments be fair and impartial. He saw these aims as part of a transformation to a more rational and enlightened society based on the social contract philosophy. In the event, they became the inspiration of a new philosophical movement for the reduction of all punishments which swiftly swept across continental Europe and eventually reached the shores of England.

All punishment is in itself evil, declared Beccaria, since it inflicts pain. It is a kind of "counter-crime" committed with the authority of the law. Hence, it should be indulged in only to exclude some greater evil. It does not exist to torture human beings or to rescind a crime already committed. It is to prevent criminals from doing further harm to society and to deter others from committing crimes.

Death Penalty and Torture

Beccaria believed that the death penalty failed to act as a deterrent and was, therefore, useless. It was itself a barbarous act of violence and injustice, since it rendered an act legitimate in payment for an equivalent act of violence. He continued that countries and times most notorious for the severity of punishments were always those in which the most bloody and inhuman actions and the most atrocious crimes were committed, for the hand of the legislator and that of the assassin were directed by the same spirit of ferocity. As for torture, whereas the Roman Catholic Church argued that torture was a mercy to the criminal since it purged him in death from the sin of falsehood, Beccaria denounced this as "a ridiculous motive for torture which should not be tolerated". A man, he said, is either guilty or not guilty of committing a crime. If shown to be guilty he should be punished according to the law and torture becomes useless as his confession is unnecessary. If he is not guilty, an innocent man is tortured to no purpose. He deplored the concept that a person should be both accuser and accused and making pain the crucible of truth, as if the test of it "lay in the muscles and sinews of an unfortunate wretch".

In order to avoid being an act of violence, he concluded, every punishment, "should be public, immediate and necessary; the least possible in the case; proportioned to the crime and determined by the law".

Impact in England

Beccaria's impact was not felt immediately in England where the defence of property was still the principal purpose of punishment. In fact, the second half of the 18th-century witnessed a strengthening of the penal laws and an extension in the incidence of the death penalty.

It is true, of course, that England had the advantage of trial by jury and the lack of the torture and secret trials that existed on the continent. But the plight of prisoners (who were unconvicted defendants) was grim indeed. They languished in appalling plague-infested conditions in prison before trial and when brought into court were not allowed counsel to represent them with the result that many were transported or sent to the gallows with no recognisable form of trial at all. They were often illiterate, disease-ridden and overawed by the pageantry of the court and the judge so that they were speechless when their lives depended upon a vigorous defence. Rules of evidence hardly existed and the pre-modern trial was "brutally rapid". Even later one writer explained how the situation had not changed:

> Fifty or sixty prisoners are kept in readiness in the dock under the court, to be brought up as they may be called for. These men, seeing their fellow prisoners return tried and found guilty in a minute or two ... become so alarmed and nervous ... that ... they lose all command over themselves, and are then, to use their own language, taken up to be knocked down like bullocks, unheard. Full two thirds of the prisoners, on their return from their trials, cannot tell of anything which has passed in the court; not even, very frequently, whether they have been tried; and it is not, indeed, uncommon for a man to come back, after receiving his sentence on the day appointed for that purpose, saying, "It can't be me they mean; I have not been tried yet."[1]

However, the influence of Beccaria resulted in a greater awareness of injustice and the gradual improvement in the situation. The lawyers who adopted his principles created a revolution in criminal law that commenced the birth and growth of the modern concept of human rights.

In his great treatise on English law Sir William Blackstone merely mentioned Beccaria in passing (but Beccaria's book had been published only the year before) and even believed that punishment should be increased where temptation was greater—presumably as a deterrent. Thus theft of a handkerchief from the person should result in death, whilst theft of a more

---

1. Thomas Wontner (1833), *Old Bailey Experience: Criminal Jurisprudence and the Actual Working of Our Penal Code of Laws*, London, pp. 59-60. Cited by John H Langbein (2003), *The Origins of Adversary Criminal Trial*, Oxford: Oxford University Press, p. 318.

valuable load of hay merited transportation.² Nevertheless, he did complain about the extent of capital punishment and, with Beccaria, argued that the certainty of punishment was a greater deterrent than its severity. Moreover, Sir William Holdsworth argues that it was Beccaria's influence "which helped to give a more critical tone to his treatment of the English criminal law than to his treatment of any other part of English law".³

Influence on Law Reformers

Bentham was the first in England to acknowledge full-blown support for Beccaria's principles. "Oh my master", he cried,

> first evangelist of Reason, you who have raised your Italy so far above England and I would add above France ... You who have made so many useful excursions into the path of utility, what is there left for us to do? — Never to turn aside from that path.⁴

Bentham too was totally opposed to the death penalty (see *Chapter 10*) and with Beccaria he considered all punishment an evil which should be imposed only if it promised to exclude some greater evil. Like Beccaria he believed that the value of the punishment should be sufficient only to outweigh the profit of the offence.

That great criminal law reformer, Samuel Romilly, acknowledged a debt to Beccaria in his first speech in the House of Commons on criminal law reform. And, in 1771, William Eden, later Lord Auckland, published *Principles of Penal Law*, in which he sought to win support for the ideals of Beccaria by advocating that vindictive justice was utterly appalling. He held that severe penalties were the instruments of despotism and that punishments that were too severe led to impunity. The infliction of death, he wrote, was not a proper mode of punishment but should be a last resort, in the case of absolute necessity, in clearing from society those who threatened public safety. In

---

2. Sir William Blackstone (1809 edn.), *Commentaries on the Laws of England*, vol. iv. London, Cadell.
3. Sir William Holdsworth. (1938), *A History of English Law*, London: Methuen & Co. Ltd.
4. A.P d'Entrèves. (1964), Introduction to Alessandro Manzoni's *The Column of Infamy:* Prefaced by Cesare Beccaria's *Of Crimes and Punishments*, London: Oxford University Press, p. x.

words reminiscent of Beccaria, he said, "Penal laws are to check the arm of wickedness, but not to wage war with the natural sentiments of the heart".[5]

Eden was supported by Romilly who had an even more significant impact in inspiring a generation of law reformers, who ultimately achieved a revolutionary breakthrough in England in the mid-19th-century when the death penalty was abolished for all but the crimes of murder and treason. Not least among the reformers who helped bring that about were the Criminal Law Commissioners appointed by Lord Brougham (*Chapter 6*) in 1833 a year after the passing of the Great Reform Act. It was through all these pioneers of criminal law reform that the principles of Beccaria were absorbed into England's criminal justice system.

Lessons for Today

The perception and reasoning of Beccaria about the need for humanity in criminal law and the role of the Rule of Law as a binding force in society reveal the genius of a book that still has many lessons for the lawyers and legislators of 21st-century Britain. At a time when civil liberties are being threatened by the belief of many men in power that anti-terrorist laws should take precedence, human rights and the Rule of Law must prevail.

Sharp disagreements on the purposes of punishment and the function of prisons continue today. In many parts of the world the use of capital punishment and forms of torture is again exercising the minds and passions of many people. Beccaria pointed the way forward with his fervent opposition to arbitrary rule, cruelty and intolerance and made clear the proper role of the criminal justice system. The perception and reasoning of Beccaria about the need for humanity in the criminal law and the function of the Rule of Law as a binding force in society still have many lessons for lawyers, criminologists and many others in modern-day Britain.

---

5. William Eden. (1771), *Principles of Penal Law*, London: B White and T Cadell, pp. 12, 14.

Select Bibliography

A

A Compleat Collection of State Tryals for High Treason. (1719) 4 vols.

Adams, Charles Francis. (1856) *The Works of John Adams, second President of the United States, with a life of the author, notes and illustrations.* Boston: Little Brown. vols. ii and vii.

Agar, Herbert. (1965) *Abraham Lincoln.* London: Collins.

Atlay, J. B. (1906) *The Victorian Chancellors.* London: Smith Elder & Co., vol. i. pp.375-6.

B

Barker, Sir Ernest. (1928 edn.) *Political Thought in England, 1848-1914.* Oxford: Oxford University Press.

Basler, Roy P. (ed.) (1946) *Abraham Lincoln: His Speeches and Writings.* New York: Da Capo Press.

Beccaria, Cesare. (1880 edn.) *Of Crimes and Punishments. (Dei Delitti e delle Pene)* Translated by J. A. Farrer. London: Chatto & Windus.

Bentham, Jeremy. (1830) *Rationale of Punishment.* In *Works.* London: Athlone Press.

(1791) *Codification Proposal Addressed to All Nations Professing Liberal Opinions. Works.* London: John Bowring. vol. iv.

(1791) *The Influence of Time and Place in Matters of Legislation. Works.* London: John Bowring. vol. i.

(1791) *Panopticon or The Inspection House. Works.* London: John Bowring. vol. iv.

Berry, D. H. (2008) *Cicero: Defence Speeches.* Oxford: Oxford University Press.

Birkenhead, Earl of. (no date) *Famous Trials.* London: Hutchinson & Co.

Birkett, Lord. (1961) *Six Great Advocates.* London: Penguin Books.

Blackstone, Sir William. (1809 edn.) *Commentaries on the Laws of England.* vol. iv. London: T. Cadell.

Block, Brian P. and Hostettler, John. (2002) *Famous Cases: Nine Trials that Changed the Law.* Sherfield-on-Loddon: Waterside Press.

Bracton, Henry de. (c. 1250) *De Legibus Et Consuetudinibus.* (Of the Laws and Customs of England). Lib. Iii. F. 118.

Brougham, Henry. (1838) *Speeches.* Edinburgh.

(1871) *The Life and Time of Henry, Lord Brougham.* London: W. Blackwood & Sons.

C

Cicero, Marcus Tullius. (1896) *Pro Cluentio.* (ed. J. D. Maillard) London: W. B. Clive.

(1999) *On the Commonwealth and On the Laws.* (ed. James E. G. Zetzel) Cambridge: Cambridge University Press.

Cobbett, William. (1809) *State Trials.*

Coke, Sir Edward. (1600-1642) *Reports.* Dublin: J. Moore.

(1779) *2-4 Institutes.* London: E. & R. Brooke.

(1823) *1 Institute—Littleton.* 2 vols. (with notes by Francis Hargrave, Charles Butler, Hale (LCJ) and Nottingham (LCJ)).

Criminal Law Review. (1960)

D

Darrow, Clarence. (1957) Speeches in *Attorney For the Damned.* (ed. Arthur Weinberg) London: Macdonald.

Denning, Lord. (1979) *The Discipline of Law.* London: Butterworths.

(1982) *What Next in the Law.* London: Butterworths.

D'Entrèves, A. P. (1964) Introduction to Alessandro Manzoni's *The Column of Infamy:* Prefaced by Cesare Beccaria's *Of Crimes and Punishments,* London: Oxford University Press.

Donald, David Herbert. (1995) *Lincoln.* London: Jonathan Cape.

E

Eden, William. (1771) *Principles of Penal Law.* London: B. Wight and T. Cadell.

Emlyn, Sollom. (1736) Preface to Matthew Hale's *The History of the Pleas of the Crown.* London: E. and R. Nutt and R. Gosling. vol. 1.

Everitt, Anthony. (2003) *Cicero, The Life and Times of Rome's Greatest Politician.* New York: Random House Trade Paperbacks.

F

Feldman, Paul H. (1997) *Jack the Ripper: The Final Chapter.* London: Virgin Books.
Foot, Paul. (1989) "Whitehall Farce". *London Review of Books.*
Ford, Trowbridge H. (1995) *Henry Brougham and His world. A Biography.* Chichester: Barry Rose.
Freeman, Iris. (1993) *Lord Denning: A Life.* London: Hutchinson.

G

Gardiner, S. R. (1894) *History of the Commonwealth and Protectorate, 1649-1660.* Vol. i.
Grant, Michael. (1965) *Cicero Selected Works.* London: Penguin Books.

H

Hansard. (1887).
Hargrave. (1665) *Tracts.* BL. *Add. MSS.* 18,234.
Hart, H. A. L. (1982) *Essays on Bentham. Studies in Jurisprudence and Political Theory.* Oxford: Clarendon Press.
Himmelfarb, Gertrude. (1968) "The Haunted House of Jeremy Bentham". In *Victorian Minds.* London: Weidenfeld & Nicolson.
Holdsworth, Sir William. (1965) *A History of English Law.* London: Methuen & Co. Ltd. Sweet and Maxwell. vols. vi and xv.
Hostettler, John. (1992) *The Politics of Criminal Law: Reform in the Nineteenth Century.* Chichester: Barry Rose Law Publishers.
  (1995) *Politics and Law in the Life of Sir James Fitzjames Stephen.* Chichester: Barry Rose Law Publishers.
  (1997) *Sir Edward Carson—A Dream Too Far.* Chichester: Barry Rose Law Publishers.
  (2010) with Richard Braby. *Sir William Garrow: His Life, Times and Fight for Justice.* Sherfield-on-Loddon: Waterside Press.
  (2010) *Thomas Erskine and Trial by Jury.* Sherfield-on-Loddon: Waterside Press.

House of Commons Journals. Vol. vii.

Howell, T. (1812) *State Trials.*

Humphreys, Sir Travers. (1955) *A Book of Trials. Personal Recollections of an Eminent Judge of the High Court.* London: Pan Books Ltd.

Hyde, H. Montgomery. (1953) *Carson. The Life of Sir Edward Carson, Lord Carson of Duncairn.* London: Hamish Hamilton.

(1964) *Norman Birkett. The Life of Lord Birkett of Ulverston.* London: Hamish Hamilton.

I

Ilbert, Sir Courtenay. (1894) "Sir James Stephen as a Legislator". 10 *Law Quarterly Review,* p. 224.

Irvine, H. B. (1927) *The Trial of Mrs. Maybrick.*

J

Jaffa, Harry V. (2000) *A New Birth of Freedom: Abraham Lincoln and the Coming of the Civil War.* Lanham, MD: Rowman and Littlefield.

Johnson, Paul. (1997) *A History of the American People.* London: Weidenfeld & Nicolson.

Justice of the Peace Reports. (1993) vol. 157.

K

Kidder, Frederick. (1870) *History of the Boston Massacre.* Albany: New York Joel Munsell.

L

Langbein, John H. (2003) *The Origins of Adversary Criminal Trial.* Oxford: Oxford University Press.

Law Journal. (1895) vol. xxx. p. 393.

Law Magazine and Law Review. (1864-5) vol. 18. p. 139.

Le Marchant, Sir Denis. 'Diary'. (30 November 1830). In Arthur Aspinall. (1952) *Three Early Nineteenth Century Diaries.* London: Williams & Norgate.

Lincoln, Abraham. (1990) *Speeches and Writings.* New York: Da Capo Press.

Lord Lloyd of Hampstead. (1979) *Introduction to Jurisprudence.* London: Stevens & Sons.

M

McCullough, David. (2001) *John Adams.* New York: Simon & Schuster Paperbacks.
MacDougall, Alexander. (1891) *The Maybrick Case.* London: Bailliere, Tindal & Cox.
MacGregor, Neil. (2011) *A History of the World in 100 Objects.* London: Allen Lane.
McLaren, Angus. (1995) *A Prescription for Murder: The Victorian Serial Killings of Dr Thomas Neill Cream.* Chicago, University of Chicago Press.
Maybrick, Florence. (1905) *My Fifteen Lost Years.* New York and London: Funk & Wagnalls.
Mill, John Stuart. (August 1838) "Bentham". *London and Westminster Review.*
Murphy, Cait. (2010) *Scoundrels in Law: The Trials of Howe & Hummel, Lawyers to the Gangsters, Cops, Starlets, and Rakes who made the Gilded Age.* New York: Harper Collins Publishers.

N

New York Tribune. (2 September 1902).

O

Old Bailey Proceedings. (www.oldbaileyonline.org. 18 September 1854) Ref: t18540918-997.

P

Peirce, Gareth. (2010) *Dispatches from the Dark Side: On Torture and the Death of Justice.* London: Verso.
Phillipson, P. (1923) *Three Criminal Law Reformers. Beccaria, Bentham, Romilly.* London: J. M. Dent & Sons Limited.

R

Roberts, Clayton. (1966) *The Growth of Responsible Government in Stuart England.*
Robertson, Geoffrey. (1998) *The Justice Game.* London: Chatto & Windus.
 (2005) *The Tyrannicide Brief: The Story of the Man who sent Charles I to the Scaffold.* London: Chatto & Windus.
 (2009) Website. www.geoffreyrobertson.com

Rovere, Richard H. (1948) *Howe & Hummel: Their True and Scandalous History.* London: Michael Joseph.

Rubinstein, Ronald. (1948) *John Citizen and the Law.* West Drayton: Penguin Books.

Rubinstein, Christopher R. (1958) *John Citizen and the Law.* 4th edition, Harmondsworth: Penguin Books. (1963) 5th edition.

S

Sandburg, Carl. (1926) *Abraham Lincoln. The Prairie Years.* London: Jonathan Cape.

Smith, Sydney. (1825) "Bentham's Book of Fallacies". *Edinburgh Review.* vol. xiii. p.367.

Stephen, Sir James Fitzjames. (1863 and 1890) *A General View of the Criminal Law of England.* London and Cambridge: Macmillan & Co.

   (1873) *Liberty, Equality, Fraternity.* London: Smith, Elder & Co.

   (1883) *A History of the Criminal Law of England.* 3 vols. London: Macmillan.

Stephen Family. Letters and Papers. University of Cambridge Library. Add. 7349.

Stewart Robert. (1986) *Henry Brougham: His Public Career—1778-1868.* London: The Bodley Head.

Stone, Irving. (1949) *Darrow For the Defence.* London: The Bodley Head.

T

The Times. (December 1812).

Train, Arthur. (1908) *True Stories of Crime From the District Attorney's Office.* London: T. Werner Laurie.

V

Vogler, Richard. (2005) *A World View of Criminal Justice.* Aldershot: Ashgate Publishing Ltd.

W

Wedgwood, C. V. (1964) *Thomas Wentworth: First Earl of Strafford 1593-1641. A Revaluation.* London: Jonathan Cape.

Who's Who. (2010)

Wontner, Thomas. (1883) *Old Bailey Experience: Criminal Jurisprudence and the Actual Working of our Penal Code of Laws.* London.

Twenty Famous Lawyers

Index

A

abortion *93, 161*
Adams, John *73–80, 134*
Admiralty *34*
admiration *67*
adultery *67, 124*
adversary trial *134*
advocacy *25, 47, 48, 66, 94, 98, 114, 162*
age of criminal responsibility *142*
Alderley *47*
Alfred the Great *133*
alibi *83, 173*
al-Qaida *175*
Amnesty International *111*
Amsterdam *77*
Andover Grammar School *177*
Anglo-Saxon England *133*
anti-social behaviour orders *142*
Antony, Mark *64*
Archer-Shee, George *34*
argument *58*
Armstrong, William "Duff" *115*
Arpinum (Arpino) *57*
arsenic *93, 154–157, 163*
assassination *119*
Assizes *91, 92, 148*
asylum *141*
Attorney-General *67, 121*
Australia *105, 147, 153*
    Western Australia *153*
Austria *162, 186*
authoritarianism *xi*
Avory, Mr Justice *89*

B

Bacon murders (Bacon, Thomas) *148*
bail *121, 138*
Bancroft, Archbishop *125*
Bankes, Eldon *32*
banknote *108*
barbarity *99*
Barnum, PT *44*
barristers as actors *162*
Barrow, Eliza *163*
Barrow-in-Furness Grammar School *87*
Barrymore, John *44*
Bath Club *89*
Battered Skull *26*
beautiful speaking voice *167*
Beccaria, Cesare *75, 96, 135, 185–190*
Bedford Gaol *91*
Begg, Moazzam *174*
Belfast *37*
benefit of clergy *52*
Bentham, Jeremy *95–104, 185, 189*
Bentley Wood High School *141*
Bethnal Green *164*
Bettaney, Michael *84*
bias *58*
big business *31*

bigotry *13*
Bill of Rights *186*
Bingham, Lord *177*
Birkett, Norman *87–94*
Birmingham Assizes *32*
Birmingham Six *174, 182*
Birnberg, Benedict *171*
biting off of ears *136*
black defendants *182*
blackmail *44, 45*
Blackstone *114, 188*
blasphemy *106–107, 110*
Blazing Car Murder *91*
Bloody Code *186*
Bogdanov, Michael *107*
Boggs, Stephen *108*
bon vivants, etc. *39*
Boston Massacre *75*
Bournville *32*
Bow Street Magistrates' Court *165*
Bracton *123*
Bradshaw, John *49*
Braintee *80*
Braintree (Quincy), New England *73*
branding *135*
Branson, Mr Justice *92*
Breda *101*
Brennan, John *27*
Brenton, Howard *107*
bribery *13, 44, 58*
Brides-in-the-Bath *164*
Brighton *83, 161*
  Brighton Bombing *83*
  Brighton Trunk Murder *92*
Bright's disease *159*

brilliance *14*
British Film Institute *144*
brothel-keeping *39*
Brougham, Henry (Lord Brougham)
  65–72, 95, 190
brutality *121*
Bryan, William Jennings *20*
bullying *95*
Burnham, Alice *165*
Burnham, Andy *144*
Bury St Edmunds *47, 53*

C

Cadbury's *31*
  Cadbury, John *33*
  Cadbury, William *32*
Caesar, Julius *62–63*
Calvin's Case *50*
Cambridge *87, 94, 121, 159, 161*
Canada *147*
  Criminal Code of Canada *152*
capital punishment *vii, 17, 27, 52, 84, 98,*
  106, 111, 134, 150, 153, 164, 179,
  185, 187
caprice *136*
Carson, Edward *25–38*
Catherine the Great *186*
Catiline Orations *62*
Cavendish, Lord Frederick *27*
Central Criminal Court *71*
Central London Property Trust Ltd v. High
  Trees House Limited *178*
Chakrabati, Shami *141–146*
Chancery *123*
change *ix, 160*

Charles I *49*, *111*
Charles II *50*, *111*
Charlottesville *138*
Charter 88 *85*
Cheltenham Ladies' College *171*
Chicago *15*, *116*
China *159*
Cicero, Marcus Tullius *57–64*
civil
    civil cases *44*
    civil disobedience *86*
    civil liberties *viii*, *81*, *105*, *141*, *182*, *190*
    civil rights *171*
        Civil Rights Movement *23*
    civil war *37*, *47*, *113*, *133*
        American Civil War *114–118*
Clapham Sect *97*
clarity *97*
class *96–97*
Clegg, Nick *144*
clemency *64*
cleverness *44*
Clifford's Inn *121*
Cobbett, William *66*
codification *96*, *147*, *150*
    Draft Criminal Code for England *152*
coercion *147*, *152*
    "Coercion Carson" *25*
    Coercive Acts *133*
Coke, Edward *74*, *121–130*, *133*
colonies *147*
Combe v. Combe *178*
Common Law *viii*, *48*, *54*, *97*, *121*, *132*, *178*
    supremacy of the Common Law *128*

Communism *14*, *15*, *91*, *110*
compensation *101*, *137*
Confederate States *116*
confession *18*, *84*, *111*, *122*, *174*, *187*
Conlon, Gerry *83*
conscience *159*
consideration *178*
conspiracy *26*, *62*, *85*
constitutional law *105*
Constitution of Massachusetts *78*
controversy *147*
Cooke, Alistair *136*
Cooke, John *111*
corruption *59*, *60*, *173*
counter-crime
    99, *187*
county courts *71*
Court of Appeal *52*, *84*, *94*, *107*, *165*, *173*, *178*, *180*
Court of Common Pleas *122*
Court of Criminal Appeal *157*
Court of King's Bench *35*, *49*, *124*
crime
    Crimes Act 1887 (Ireland) *25*
    crimes against humanity *94*
criminal
    Criminal Cases Review Commission *173*
    criminal law *105*
    Criminal Law Commissioners *96*, *190*
Cromwell, Oliver *47*, *111*
cross-examination *x*, *26*, *32*, *35*, *89*, *91*, *108*
Crouch, Harriet *93*
cruelty *102*, *185*
    cruel and unusual punishments *138*

Curragh Mutiny *37*
Czechoslovakia *111*

D
Darling, Charles *28*
Darling, Mr Justice *165*
Darrow, Clarence *vii*, *13–23*
Davis, David *144*
Davis, Jefferson *117*
Dayton, Tennessee *20*
death sentence *98*, *134*, *150*, *153*, *164*, *185*, *187*
Declaration of Independence (USA) *73–77*, *116*, *131*
defence *60*
   million-dollar defence *19*
De Meneze, John Charles *174*
democracy *viii*, *ix*, *47*, *64*, *85*
Denning, Alfred (Lord Denning) *vii*, *177–184*
Derby Assizes *158*
despotism *189*
detention without charge *142*
Detroit *21*
diplomacy *118*, *131*
disablement *102*
disclosure *84*, *174*
discrimination *85*, *142*
disfiguring *136*
dismembering *135*
dispensations *136*
Disraeli *152*
dissent *81*
Dodge-Morse case *45*
Donaldson, Mr Justice *83*

Donegal *26*
double jeopardy *137*
Doughty Street Chambers *82*, *106*
Douglas, Lord Alfred *30*
D'Oyly Carte, Richard *29*
DPP v. Smith *179*
Drabble, Margaret *107*
Dred Scott v. Sandford *116*
Drew, John *44*
Drury, Kenneth *173*
Dublin *25*, *27*
   Trinity College Dublin *28*
due process *137*

E
Earl of Essex *121*
Earl of Southampton *121*
Earl of Strafford *48*
East India Company *149*
Eden, William *189*
Edinburgh University *159*
Edward VIII *93*
Ellenborough, Lord *66*
eloquence *17*, *57*, *168*
Elwes, Richard *91*
energy *80*
Enlightenment *74*, *102*, *132*, *186*
equality *116*, *118*, *141*
   substantial equality *152*
equity *178*
Erskine, Thomas *x*, *68*, *74*
espionage *84*
Essex Street Chambers (No.39) *141*
estoppel *179*
ethics *86*

Europe *185*
    European Convention on Human Rights *86*
    European Court of Human Rights *105, 110*
Eve Was Framed *85*
evidence *x, 58, 76, 188*
    fabrication *44, 183*
    rules of evidence *149*
    tampering with *174*
evil *99, 107, 114, 135, 149*
    government a necessary evil *152*
    greater evil *187*
    punishment evil *187*
evolution *19*
Exeter Assizes *158*
exile *63*
extortion *58, 60*
extraordinary rendition *142*

F

facts *76*
fair comment *29*
fair trial *75, 142, 148, 155, 186*
Fawkes, Guy *121*
fear *185*
    fearlessness *13*
ferocity *187*
Finch, Atticus *142*
Fleet Gaol *125*
flogging *31, 66*
Flying Squad *173*
folklore *45*
force *152*
forensics *161*

forensic giants *20*
Forgery and Counterfeiting Act 1981 *108*
Founding Fathers (USA) *128–130, 136*
France *77*
Franklin, Benjamin *77, 134*
fraternity *147, 152*
fraud *93*
freedom *121, 147, 186*
    freedom of speech *16, 79, 127, 142*
    free press *66*
freezing injunction *180*
French, Dr Frank *164*
French Revolution *x, 97*
Fry, Elizabeth *101*
Fuller, Nicholas *125*
Fuller's Case *125*

G

gangsters *14*
Garrow, William *x, 149*
general good *152*
genius *161*
George III *67*
George IV *67*
Gettysburgh Address *118*
Gilbert, W S *28*
Glasgow *82*
Gloucestershire *47*
Glover v. Bishop of Coventry *124*
gouging out of eyes *136*
Government of Ireland Act 1922 *37*
Grand Duke Leopold *186*
Grant, Ulysses *118*
Gray's Inn *82*
Great Reform Act 1832 *97, 190*

greed *57*
Green Bicycle Murder *87, 167*
Gregory, Maundy *93*
gross indecency *107*
Grosvenor Square *45*
Guantánamo Bay *142, 174*
Guildford Four *83, 174, 182*
gunpowder plot *121*
Gweedore *26*

H

habeas corpus 121, 125, 129
Hale, Matthew *47–56, 133*
    Hale Commission *52*
Hamilton, Duke of *49*
Hammersmith *68*
happiness *96, 102, 135*
Hardin County, Kentucky *114*
harm *187*
Harrison, Peachy *115*
Harrow *141*
Harrow Weald Sixth Form College *141*
Harvard *73*
    Harvard Law School *18*
Hastings, Warren *74*
Hatful of Oranges *69*
Hatry, Clarence *93*
Hatton, Lady *129*
Havel, Vaclav *110*
Havers, Michael *107*
Hawkins, William *74*
Hearn, Sarah *93*
hearsay *98*
Hebel, Judge Oscar *16*
Henn Collins, Mr Justice *30*

Henry III *124*
Hermann, Marie *162*
Herne Bay *164*
hierarchy *58*
High Commission *124*
High Court *50, 87, 89, 94, 110, 153, 178*
High Trees House *178*
history *47*
histrionics *ix, 161*
hoaxes *42*
Holdsworth, William *55, 149, 189*
Holland *77*
    Panoptican *101*
Home Office *141*
Home Rule *36*
Home Secretary *153*
honesty *80*
honours scandal *93*
horror *185*
Hortensius *60, 169*
Houndsditch *95*
House of Lords *67, 70, 82, 94, 105, 107, 165, 178*
    reform *86*
Howard, John *100–101*
Howe, William *40–46*
Hughes, Robert *109*
human freedom *17*
humanism *vii*
humanity *14, 60, 186, 190*
human rights *viii, 82, 105, 141, 175*
    European Convention on Human Rights *86*
    Human Rights Act 1998 *141*
Hummel, Abraham *41–46*

Humphries, Abbie *84*
Hutchinson, Jeremy *107*
hysteria *17*

I

identity cards *142*
ignorance *13*
Ilbert, Courtenay *151*
Illinois *17*
impartiality *186*
impeachment *48, 74, 125, 134*
imprisonment *102*
incitement *44*
independent spirit *74*
India *96, 147, 149, 158*
infant prodigy *95*
inheritance *59*
'Inherit the Wind' *21*
Inner Temple *87, 121, 148*
inquisitorial system *x, 185*
Institutes of the Law of England *123*
integrity *54*
intuition *26*
IRA *83*
Ireland *25, 111*
Irving, Henry *28, 44*
Isaacs, Rufus *32, 163*
Isle of Wight *34*
Israeli Embassy bombing *85*

J

Jack the Ripper *158*
Jefferson, Thomas *73, 77, 128, 131–139*
Jerome, William *45*
Johnson, Samuel *147*

judges *vii, 47, 79, 94, 124, 150, 153*
    The People's Judge *183*
Judicial Committee of the Privy Counci *71*
jurisprudence *69, 95, 149*
jurists *47, 121*
jury *vii, 16, 27, 36, 61, 75, 79, 92, 134, 138, 162, 188*
    jury packing *182*
    special jury *25, 32, 89*
    swaying the mind of a jury *94*
justice *ix, 28, 68, 102, 175*
    belief in justice *13*
    justice should be swift *136*
    violation of justice *54*
Just Law *85*

K

Kansas-Nebraska Act 1854 *115*
Kaye, Violette *92*
Keble, Mr Justice *51*
Keeler, Christine *179*
Kelley, Julie *84*
Kennedy, Helena *81–86*
    Helena Kennedy Foundation *82*
Kennedy, Ludovic *173*
Kensal Green *159*
Kensington *147*
Khomeini, Ayatollah *110*
kidnap *84*
King, Martin Luther *142, 171*
Kirkup, James *106*
knives *27*

L

Land League *25*
Langtry, Lily *44, 90*
Laud, William *48*
law *25, 31, 47, 57, 95, 114, 149, 152*
    artificiality *97*
    complexity *97*
    contempt for *99*
    criminal law *95*
    irrationality *97*
    Law Amendment Society *71*
    law reform *54, 66, 69*
    manipulation of the law *42*
    Mohammedan law *149*
    obscurity of the law *97*
    science of law *97*
Lawrence, Geoffrey *94*
Lawton, Mr Justice *28*
lawyers
    trial lawyers *xi*
Lee, Robert E *118*
legend *13, 42*
Leicester Assizes *167*
leniency *99*
Leopold, Nathan *17*
Leveson, Lord Justice *145*
    Leveson Inquiry *145*
Levin, Bernard *107*
Lewes *92*
libel *31, 89, 93*
liberty *ix, 14, 111, 128, 133, 147*
    Liberty, Equality, Fraternity *147, 152*
Liberty *141*
Libya *145*
lies *84*

Light, Ronald *167*
Lilburne, John *111*
limelight *94, 171*
Lincoln, Abraham *113–120*
    third-rate lawyer *113*
Lincoln Assizes *148*
Lincoln's Inn *48, 95, 156, 177*
Lipski, Israel *153*
literature *147*
Liverpool Assizes *155*
Lloyd George *25*
Lloyd, William *16*
Loeb, Richard *17*
Lofty, Margaret *165*
logic *97*
London *79, 163*
    London School of Economics *141, 145, 171*
    London University *148*
loopholes *41*
Lord Chancellor *69, 125, 156*
Louisiana *134*
Love, Christopher *50*
Lush, Mr Justice *165*
Luton Post Office Murder *173*
lynching *14*

M

Macaulay, Thomas Babington *96, 149*
MacDougall, Alexander *156*
MacMahon, Joseph *27*
MacNeill, Mr Justice *108*
Magdalen Hall, Oxford *48*
Magee, Patrick *83*
magistrates *150*

Magna Carta 128
magnetic quality 167
maiming 136
Malawi 111
malpractice 96
Mancini, Tony 92
Mansfield College 81
manslaughter 26, 39, 76, 150, 161
Marchioness 174
Mareva Injunction 180
Marquess of Queensberry 30
Marshall Hall, Edward 29, 87, 161–170
Marshall, John 79
Martin, Thomas 27
Massachusetts 73, 76
Master of the Rolls 178
Matrimonial Homes Act 1967 181
Matrix Chambers 145
Maybrick, Florence 154
Maybrick, James 158
"Mayfair Playboys" 93
McFadden, Father 26
media 20, 85, 175
medieval criminal law 185
mercy 18, 28, 68, 76, 136, 187
Merriman, Boyd (Lord Merriman) 89
Methodism 97
MI5 84
Michael X 110
Middle Temple 71, 106, 144
Midland Circuit 31, 148
Milan 185
Mill, James 96
Mill, John Stuart 98, 152
Milwaukee 16

miscarriages of justice 172, 182
Mohammedan law 149
Monke, General 53
Monkey Trial 19
morality 31, 90, 101–104, 106, 147, 149, 152
Mortimer, John 106
Mothers Behind Bars 85
motive 92, 102, 155
Mountbatten, Lady 93
Mozambique 111
Munday, Bessie 164
murder 18, 26, 39, 58, 63, 76, 87, 115, 153, 161, 173, 182
   murder by the state 185
   murder most foul 183
Murena, Lucius 62
Muslims 175

N

Napoleon 80
National Theatre 107
natural rights 134
necessity 189
negligence 150
New Model Army 50
New Salem, Illinois 114
newspapers 154
New York 39
New Zealand 147, 152
Nonconformists 82
Norfolk 121, 129
Northampton 91
Nottingham 90
Notting Hill 172

Nuremberg War Trials *87, 94*

O
oath *126*
obscenity *107*
Official Secrets Act 1911 *84*
Ohio *13*
Old Bailey *x, 40, 85, 106, 107, 111, 153, 162, 165, 174*
    Old Bailey lawyers *149*
On Crimes and Punishments *75, 185*
opium *158*
    Opium War *159*
oppression *15, 127*
Orange Order *37*
oratory *94, 169*
Osborne *34*
outspoken *13*
Oxford *48, 82, 84, 95, 105, 159, 171, 177*
    Oxford Brookes University *141*

P
Pace, Beatrice *93*
pain *187*
Palles, Chief Baron *27*
Palmer, Jackson *93*
Panopticon *100*
pardon *17, 51, 186*
Paris *79*
Parliament *100*
    Parliament Act 1911 *36*
    sovereignty of Parliament *111*
partiality *156*
passion *13*
paternalism *96*

Peacham, Edmund *126*
Peel, Robert *186*
Peirce, Gareth *171–176*
penal servitude *26, 157, 162*
Pennsylvania *135*
perjury *44, 45, 111*
personal flaws *viii*
persuasion *viii, 58, 152, 169*
Peterborough Cathedral *106*
petition *51*
    Petition of Right *35, 128*
Philadelphia *77, 136*
philanthropy *33, 96*
philosophy *57, 95*
Phoenix Park *27*
phone-hacking *145*
pickets *14*
Pickford, Mr Justice *32*
pillory *135*
Pinkerton detectives *14*
Pleas of the Crown *55*
poison *161–164*
police *84, 158, 174*
    Police and Criminal Evidence Act 1984 *174*
Political Register *66*
politics *vii, viii, 25, 31, 37, 47, 58, 68, 87, 114, 121, 131, 142, 151, 152*
Poole Council *144*
Poor Law *71, 101*
Portugal *186*
power *38, 97*
Prague *110*
prejudice *22, 165, 181*
press *31, 154*

Index

free press *79*
pressing to death *52*
Preston *50*
presumption of innocence *x*
Price, Richard *74*
Prince Regent *66*
Princess Caroline of Brunswick *67*
prison *100*, *188*
private prosecution *106*
Privy Council *105*
pro bono *106*
Profumo Affair *179*
proportionality *187*
prostitution *162*
Protestantism *37*
pugnacity *26*
punishment *95*, *187*
    certainty of *136*, *189*
Puritanism *47*, *125*
Putnam, John *74*

Q

Quakers *31*
Queen Mary, University of London *106*
Queen's evidence *173*
Queensland *153*
Queen's Medical Centre, Nottingham *84*
quixotic *13*

R

racial hatred *14*, *21*
radical lawyers *171*
Raleigh, Walter *121*
rancour *121*
Randolph, Jan *131*

rape *136*
Reading Gaol *31*
Reading, Lord Chief Justice *165*
rebellion *127*, *150*
reform *54*, *66*, *69*, *85*, *95*, *180*, *190*
    Great Reform Act 1832 *70*, *190*
    reformation of offenders *100*
Regulation of Investigatory Powers Act of 2000 *144*
religion *147*, *152*
    Nonconformists *82*
    religious extremism *47*
    religious toleration *53*
reprieve *153*
respect *141*
restorative justice *x*
retribution *148*
revenge *149*
revolution *68*, *73*, *132*
rhetoric *57*
Ridley, Mr Justice *35*
rights *64*, *133*, *137*
riot *76*
robbery *93*
Robertson, Geoffrey *105–112*
"Romans in Britain" *107*
Rome *vii*, *57*, *169*
    Roman Catholicism *186*
Romilly, Samuel *96*, *99*, *185*, *189*
Roscius, Sextus *59*
Ross-Cornes, Graham *108*
rotten boroughs *70*
Rouse, Alfred Arthur *91*
royal prerogative *53*, *122*
Rubinstein, Chris *182*

Rubinstein, Ronald *181*
Rugby School *161*
Rule of Law *viii, 47, 64, 113, 128, 133, 136,*
    185, 190
    earliest times *58*
Rushdie, Salman *110*
Russell, Charles *155*
Russell, Lord John *185*
Russia *186*
Ruxton, Dr. Buck *93*
R v. Boggs *108*
R v. Light *167*

S

safeguards *85, 128*
Scandalous Vicar *47*
scepticism *13*
science *147*
Scopes Evolution Case *20*
Scotland Yard *158*
Scrutton, Mr Justice *165*
security *137*
Seddon, Frederick *163*
self-defence *76*
self-incrimination *121, 137*
separation of powers *79*
Sex Disqualification (Removal) Act 1919
    viii
showmanship *13*
Sicily *58, 60*
Sierra Leone *106*
silence
    right to silence *111, 150*
similar facts *165*
Simon, John *32*

Simpson, Wallis *93*
Singh, Rabinder *145*
slavery/abolition *ix, 66, 73, 79, 100, 113,*
    116, 159
    abolition of *71, 118*
    slave labourers *31*
    slave-like conditions *15*
    Slavery Emancipation Act 1831 *147*
small-claims court *52*
Smith, F E (Lord Birkenhead) *37, 156, 167*
Smith, George Joseph *164*
Smith, Gypsy Jim *179*
Smith, Sydney *103*
Smythe, John *107*
social
    social contract *186*
    social welfare *31*
Society of Black Lawyers *182*
sodomy *136*
Solemn League and Covenant *37*
Solicitor-General *121*
South Africa *111*
South Carolina *116*
Spain *127*
Springfield, Illinois *114*
Star Chamber *51, 123, 124*
Statute of Treason 1352 *48*
Stead, Wickham *153*
Stephen, James Fitzjames *55–56, 96, 147*
Stevens, Reginald *173*
stigma *175*
Stockdale, John *74*
Stockwell *174*
Stoke Poges *129*
Strasbourg *105*

Index

subtlety *44*
subversion *98*
suffragettes *86*
summing-up *110, 153, 156*
Supreme Court (USA) *115*
Sweden *186*
Sweet, Dr. Osian *21*
Sydney *105*

T
Taney, Chief Justice Roger B *116*
Tasmania *153*
Tennessee *19*
terror *x, 102, 149*
    anti-terror legislation *142*
    terrorism *172*
Thatcher, Margaret *83*
theatrical lawyers *44, 161*
theft *60*
Theresa, Maria *186*
threats *174*
Tittleshall *129*
To Kill a Mockingbird *142*
tolerance *190*
torture *84, 122, 127, 142, 174, 185*
Tower of London *122*
trade unions *14*
    Trades Union Congress *152*
transportation *100, 101, 114, 188*
treason *37, 48, 58, 83, 111, 121*
Tree, Herbert *28*
Trent Affair *117*
trial
    adversary trial *x, 134*
    fair trial *14*

state trials *x, 121*
tricksters *39*
Trinidad *110*
Trinity College, Cambridge *159*
Trinity College, Dublin *25*
Tuscany *186*
tyranny *15, 111*
    Tyrannicide Brief *111*

U
Ulster *25, 36*
    Ulster Volunteer Force *37*
    "Uncrowned King of Ulster" *25*
Ulverston *87*
underdog *vii*
United Nations Internal Justice Council *106*
University of Michigan *18*
Upper Court *49*
USA *vii, 13, 73, 113, 175*
    Founding Fathers *116*
    Panoptican *101*
utility *95*

V
verdict *58*
Verres, Caius *60*
victims' rights *142*
Vietnam *111*
violence *27, 57, 64, 187*
Virginia *132, 134*
Voltaire *186*

W
Wallace, Judge James B *39*

Walton Gaol *156*
Walton, Lawson QC *29*
war *152*
Ward, Judith *174*
Washington, George *73–74, 133*
Watkins, Lord Justice *110*
wealth *13*
Westminster *133*
    Westminster Hall *50*
    Westminster School *95*
Weymouth *164*
wheel *185*
whipping *135*
Whitbread, Samuel *67*
Whitchurch *177, 183*
Whitechapel *153*
Whitehall *111*
Whiteley, Cecil *167*
Wicked Shifts *67*
Wilberforce, William *147*
Wilde, Oscar *28, 30, 106*
Wilde, Serjeant *48*
Wilkes Booth, John *119*
Wilkes, Charles *118*
Williamsburg *132*
William the Conqueror *133*
Winchelsea *69*
Winchester *183*
    Winchester Castle *122*
Windsor *129*
    Windsor Castle *50*
Winsconsin *14*
Winslow Boy *36*
witchcraft *47, 53*
witnesses *44, 51, 58, 68, 91, 149, 155*

Wollstonecraft, Mary *74*
women
    burning of women *52*
    discrimination against women *85*
    women's movement *viii*
Woolsack *70*
Wright, Bella *167*
Wright, Peter *88*
Wright v. Gladstone *88*

X
xenophobia *15*

Y
Yorkshire *69*
Yorktown *79*

Also by John Hostettler

Sir William Garrow: His Life, Times and Fight for Justice
by John Hostettler and Richard Braby
With a Foreword by Geoffrey Robertson QC

A comprehensive account of lawyer William Garrow's life, career, family and connections. Sir William Garrow was born in Middlesex in 1760 and called to the Bar in 1783. He was the dominant figure at the Old Bailey from 1783 to 1793, later becoming an MP, Solicitor-General, Attorney-General and finally a judge and lawmaker within the Common Law Tradition. Sir William Garrow is a generous work in which well-known legal historian and biographer John Hostettler and family story-teller Richard Braby (a descendant of Garrow) combine their skills and experience to produce a gem of a book.

'A law book yes, but boring no, a delight to read': *Internet Law Book Reviews*

'A blockbuster of a book': *Phillip Taylor MBE of Richmond Green Chambers*

'[Hostettler and Braby's] definitive biography … is informative, entertaining and a really good read, and in the process rescues Garrow from undeserved obscurity': *Littlehampton Gazette*

Paperback & eBook | ISBN 978-1-904380-69-6 | 2011 | 352 pages

www.WatersidePress.co.uk

Also by John Hostettler

Garrow's Law: The BBC Drama Revisited
by John Hostettler.
With a Foreword by Bryan Gibson.

Takes the lid off the prime-time TV series - a must for lawyers and other viewers. For any of the five million people who saw the prime-time BBC series "Garrow's Law" this is an absorbing book. It is written by expert commentator John Hostettler who has studied Garrow extensively. The book uses the true facts on which the programme was based to compare drama and reality.

Paperback and eBook | ISBN 978-1-904380-90-0 | 2012 |132 pages

www.WatersidePress.co.uk

A History of Criminal Justice in England and Wales
by John Hostettler.

An ideal introduction charting all the main developments of criminal justice, from Anglo-Saxon dooms to the Common Law, struggles for political, legislative and judicial ascendency and the formation of the modern-day Criminal Justice System. Among a wealth of topics the book looks at the Rule of Law, the development of the criminal courts, police forces, jury, justices of the peace and individual crimes and punishments. It locates all the iconic events of criminal justice history and law reform within a wider background and context - demonstrating a wealth and depth of knowledge. 'Every student entering law school should have a copy and read it': *Criminal Law and Justice Weekly*

Paperback and eBook | ISBN 978-1-904380-51-1 | 2009 |352 pages

Also by John Hostettler

Famous Cases: Nine Trials that Changed the Law
by Brian P Block and John Hostettler.

Dissenters, Radicals, Heretics and Blasphemers: The Flame of Revolt that Shines Through English History
by John Hostettler.

In Famous Cases: Nine Trials that Changed the Law the authors have painstakingly assembled the background to a selection of leading cases in English law. From the Mareva case (synonymous with a type of injunction) to Lord Denning's classic ruling in the High Trees House case (the turning point for equitable estoppel) to that of the former Chilean head of state General Pinochet (in which the House of Lords heard the facts a second time) the authors offer a refreshing perspective to whet the appetite of general readers, students and seasoned practitioners alike concerning how the English Common Law evolves on a case by case basis by creating 'precedents'.

Paperback and eBook| ISBN 978-1-872870-34-2 | 2002 |136 pages

A certain level of dissent, protest and open debate is a central part of UK history and democratic processes. Taking key events from both the past and modern times John Hostettler demonstrates how when legitimate avenues of challenge to the actions of the state or other powerful groups become closed to people then they are bound to assert their grievances in other sometimes less acceptable ways.

'This book is a glorious Molotov cocktail to be placed in the hands of every citizen and lobbed at the status quo... A brilliant and exhilarating work. A counter to the politics of passivity': *Helena Kennedy QC*

Paperback and eBook | ISBN 978-1-904380-82-5 | 2012 | 272 pages

www.ingramcontent.com/pod-product-compliance
Lightning Source LLC
Chambersburg PA
CBHW070805230426
43665CB00017B/2489